100 THINGS TO DO IN LINCOLN BEFORE YOU DIE

100
THINGS TO DO IN
LINCOLN
BEFORE YOU
DIE

• •

GRETCHEN M. GARRISON

Copyright © 2020 by Reedy Press, LLC
Reedy Press
PO Box 5131
St. Louis, MO 63139, USA
reedypress.com

No part of this publication may be reproduced or transmitted in any form or by any means, electronic or mechanical, including photocopy, recording, or any information storage and retrieval system, without permission in writing from the publisher.

Permissions may be sought directly from Reedy Press at the above mailing address or via our website at reedypress.com.

Library of Congress Control Number: 2018945627

ISBN: 9781681061634

Design by Jill Halpin

Photo credit: All images are provided by the author unless noted.

Printed in the United States of America
20 21 22 23 24 5 4 3 2 1

We (the publisher and the author) have done our best to provide the most accurate information available when this book was completed. However, we make no warranty, guaranty, or promise about the accuracy, completeness or currency of the information provided, and we expressly disclaim all warranties, express or implied. Please note that attractions, company names, addresses, websites, and phone numbers are subject to change or closure, and this is outside of our control. We are not responsible for any loss, damage, injury, or inconvenience that may occur due to the use of this book. When exploring new destinations, please do your homework before you go. You are responsible for your own safety and health when using this book.

CONTENTS

Acknowledgments xii
Preface xiii

Food and Drink

1. Dine on Daikon at Bánhwich Café 2
2. Cheer for Teams Together at Gate 25 Bar and Restaurant 4
3. Something for Everyone at Goldenrod Pastries 6
4. Dine Down Havelock Avenue 8
5. Scream Out Ivanna Cone 9
6. Bite a Big Burger at Honest Abe's 10
7. Take a Sip at James Arthur Vineyards 12
8. Excite Your Taste Buds at the Oven 13
9. Relish Your Experience at Lazlo's Brewery and Grill 14
10. Savor a Slice at Lazzari's Pizza 16
11. Nibble on a Croissant at Le Quartier Bakery 18
12. Stay Caffeinated at The Mill 20
13. Celebrate Life at the Parthenon Greek Grill and Taverna 22
14. Eat Award-Winning Barbecue at Phat Jack's 23
15. Walk to Centrally Located Piedmont Bistro by Venue 24
16. Slow Down Dinner at Prairie Plate 26
17. Nosh in the Neighborhood at Toast 27
18. Try Beef and Cabbage Sandwiches at Runza 28
19. Order Breakfast (and Pies) All Day at Stauffer's Café & Pie Shoppe 30

20.	Chomp on Complimentary Chips and Salsa at Tico's Restaurant and Tequila Bar...	32
21.	Taste the Tradition at Valentino's...	34
22.	Elevate Your Expectations at Zipline Brewing Co.............................	36

Arts and Entertainment

23.	Sing Along at Abendmusik at First-Plymouth................................	40
24.	See a Live Show at Bourbon Theatre..	41
25.	Smile, You're at Champions Fun Center......................................	42
26.	Solve a Puzzle at Escape Room Lincoln......................................	43
27.	Jazz in June..	44
28.	Follow the Lied Center..	45
29.	Play Like a Kid at the Lincoln Children's Museum	46
30.	Feed the Goats at the Lincoln Children's Zoo................................	47
31.	Take in Local Theater at the Lincoln Community Playhouse.................	48
32.	Listen Closely to Lincoln's Symphony Orchestra............................	49
33.	Paint Yourself Silly..	50
34.	See a Show at Pinewood Bowl...	51
35.	Be a Spectator at Pinnacle Bank Arena..	52
36.	Twirl Around at the Pla Mor Ballroom	53
37.	Celebrate Fall at Roca Berry Farm	54
38.	Become a Film Critic at Mary Riepma Ross Media Arts Center	55
39.	Sing with Your Supper at Screamers Dining and Cabaret	56
40.	Feel the Blues at Zoo Bar...	57

Sports and Recreation

41.	Putt a Hole in One at Adventure Golf	60
42.	Try an Ollie at The Bay	61
43.	Watch Cars Go in Circles at Eagle Raceway	62
44.	Roll a Strike at 48 Bowl	63
45.	Become a Husker Fan	64
46.	See Some Stars at Hyde Observatory	65
47.	Practice Putting at Jim Ager Golf Course	66
48.	Check Out the Lincoln Stars	67
49.	Fuel Up for Racing at the Museum of American Speed	68
50.	Spin a Wheel at the National Museum of Roller Skating	69
51.	Practice Shooting at the Nebraska Game and Parks Outdoor Education Center	70
52.	Take a Hike to Pioneers Park Nature Center	71
53.	Catch a Fly Ball at the Saltdogs' Haymarket Park	72
54.	Imagine Pioneer Prairies at Spring Creek Prairie Audubon Center	73
55.	Slide into Summer at Star City Shores Aquatic Center	74
56.	Ponder the Beauty at Sunken Gardens	76
57.	Trek the Trails Around Town	77
58.	Climb a Wall at the UNL Outdoor Adventure Center	78
59.	Play a Match at Woods Tennis Center	79

Culture and History

60.	Learn about Bryan, Lincoln's Popular Politician, at his Former Fairview Farm	82
61.	Visit Another Culture at the Germans from Russia Museum	83

62.	Tour the Governor's Residence	84
63.	Appreciate What the West Has to Offer at the Great Plains Art Museum	85
64.	Piece Together the Past at the International Quilt Museum	86
65.	Read Local Literature at the Jane Pope Geske Heritage Room of Nebraska Authors	87
66.	Look Around Nebraska's Statehood Memorial, the Kennard House	88
67.	Act Like a Farmer at Larsen Tractor Test and Power Museum	89
68.	Appreciate Masterpieces at Kiechel Fine Art Gallery	90
69.	Be Remembered at the Kindler Hotel	92
70.	Feel Appreciation at the City of Lincoln Firefighter and Rescue Department Museum	93
71.	Create at LUX Center for the Arts	94
72.	Uncover a Fossil at Morrill Hall	95
73.	Experience the Nebraska Capitol	96
74.	Understand the State's Past at the Nebraska History Museum	97
75.	Go Under Lincoln at Robber's Cave	98
76.	Value Sheldon Museum of Art	99
77.	Stay in the City or Stay in the Country	100
78.	Stroll Through History at Wyuka Cemetery	102
79.	Honor the Military at Veterans Memorial Garden	103

Shopping and Fashion

80.	Shop Together at 3 Daughters Boutique	106
81.	Cultivate Ideas at Campbell's Nursery & Garden Center	108
82.	Pop Up Memories Through Colby Ridge	110
83.	Alter Your Life at Emsud's Clothiers	111

84.	Design Your Dream at Cooper & Co.	112
85.	Play an Instrument at Dietze Music	113
86.	Be Footloose & Fancy	114
87.	Lasso Your Inner Cowboy at the Fort	115
88.	From Nebraska Gift Shop	116
89.	Cook Gourmet at Habitat	117
90.	Find a Treasure at Funky Sister	118
91.	Support Local Producers at the Haymarket Farmers Market	120
92.	Find a New Pastime at HobbyTown	122
93.	Deck Yourself in Red at Husker Headquarters	124
94.	Show Your Personality at Jilly's Socks	125
95.	Try a Sample at Licorice International	126
96.	Read a Classic at A Novel Idea Bookstore	128
97.	Prepare for an Adventure at the Moose's Tooth	130
98.	Load Up on Adventure at Star City Motor Sports	132
99.	Smell Lincoln Scents at Wax Buffalo Candles	133
100.	Lace Up Perfect Shoes at the Lincoln Running Company	134

Suggested Itineraries 135

Activities by Season 138

Index 140

ACKNOWLEDGMENTS

Thank you …

To my Kyle for your love, support, and willingness to eat Mexican food for one week straight.

To Gabriel, Zeke, Kaylee, and Isaac. Introducing you to the world has always been my goal. Thanks for going along with my adventures and for (mostly) being happy about them. You are all my favorites.

To my parents and the rest of the Michels family, your encouragement and loving me for me means everything! Papa & Grandma—thanks for the property help, so I could keep writing!

To our family, church, homeschooling, hobby, and sports communities; God has placed us with some great people—you are appreciated!

To those who follow "Odyssey Through Nebraska," thanks for your support.

To my guinea pigs and consultants (Kyle, our kids, Mom and Dad M., Brady and Sheila, Joel and Courtney, Bryan and Jonica, Brenna, Suzy, Becky, Sarah, Patrice, Courtney N., and Roberta), thank you for being excited about my book, for trying new places, and for giving your honest opinions. This project was much more fun because you were all a part of it!

To Tim and Lisa, thank you for brainstorming with me on this project and for leading the way by writing three great Nebraska and Omaha travel books for Reedy Press. I greatly appreciate your input and friendship. Thank you also to everyone at Reedy Press who played a part in this project.

To all of the people who are behind the places featured in this book. Interviewing you in person, over the phone, or via email brought this project to life. You represent Lincoln well. I feel truly privileged to highlight these locations that you all bring to life.

Most of all, thanks to God, who strengthens me to live out His call.

• •

PREFACE

Lincoln is my hometown. Except when I was in college, I have lived within 25 minutes of downtown my entire life. Growing up, as my family participated in activities around town, I never really thought about the significance of those places we visited. That was just my life.

Now that my husband and I are raising our kids in the same community, I can appreciate the unique opportunities that Lincoln has to offer. Touring the Kennard House reminds me of the joy of taking field trips. Going to a Husker football game and sitting inside a "sea of red" is truly an outstanding experience. Screaming with my kids as we ride through the tunnel on the zoo train takes me back to my own childhood. Shopping at the same flower nursery that has been around for a century continues my grandmother's gardening tradition. My mouth waters as I think about eating the same traditional Runza sandwiches I also enjoyed during my youth.

If you also live in Lincoln, my hope is that this book will be used as a tool to further explore the many places you may have driven by but neglected to enjoy in the past. I want this book to introduce you to those locations that you may not have noticed. For those places that are familiar, I hope you appreciate their unique offerings in a new way. For those of you visiting Lincoln, I hope this book will be a worthwhile guide.

For all who hold a copy of this book, I hope you enjoy planning adventures at these places whose stories I enjoyed telling. But the places that are mentioned as "extras" are not just afterthoughts. Each of them carry its own compelling timeline. By including extras, this book highlights several hundred possibilities for you to explore in Lincoln.

Enjoy the journey!

FOOD AND DRINK

DINE ON DAIKON
AT BÁNHWICH CAFÉ

Hoang Nguyen often came to Lincoln to visit his future wife, Linh, when she was attending college. They came to appreciate the capital city. In 2012, after researching and developing their concept for a year, Hoang and Linh opened a specialty sandwich shop. His sister opened a Pho restaurant, and her mother relocated her longtime Asian grocery store to the same Saigon Plaza shopping center that houses all three.

The menu at Bánhwich Café features traditional Vietnamese bánh mi ingredients such as daikon and pork ear jam. Other sandwiches are inspired by Thai, Korean, and curry flavors. Hoang's time as an Asian fusion chef has influenced his topping offerings.

Along with 20 types of sandwiches, the restaurant is known for its bubble teas. Besides using syrups, Bánhwich includes fruit in its specialty drinks. This family is grateful for the all of the community support.

940 N. 26th St.
(402) 261-4655
banhwichcafe.com

OTHER ORIGINAL EAST ASIAN RESTAURANTS

Pho Factory
(another Saigon Plaza restaurant owned by this family)
(402) 261-3213
phofactorylincoln.com

Asian Fusion
2840 Jamie Ln.
(402) 423-8889
asianfusionlnk.com

Blue Orchid Thai Restaurant
129 N. Tenth St.
(402) 742-7250
facebook.com/
blueorchidrestaurant

Great Wall Chinese Restaurants
850 N. Seventieth St.
(402) 488-2112
greatwalllincoln.com

5701 NW First St.
(Highlands)
(402) 438-8888
highlandsgreat
walltogo.com

Imperial Palace
701 N. 27th St.
(402) 474-2688
imperialpalacene.net

Issara Cuisine
1701 Pine Lake Rd., Ste. 7
(402) 261-5594
issaracuisine.com

Ming's House
1415 N. Cotner Blvd., No. 103
(402) 466-3688
facebook.com/
MingsHouseLincoln

Shen Café
3520 Village Dr., Ste. 100
(402) 420-0487
shencafelincoln.com

2

CHEER FOR TEAMS TOGETHER
AT GATE 25 BAR AND RESTAURANT

"Through these gates pass the greatest fans in college sports." These words are etched on Gate 1 of nearby Memorial Stadium where the Huskers play football. Since there are 24 entrances, the name "Gate 25" connects football fans to this downtown destination. In 2013, this bar and restaurant was one of the first places to open in Lincoln's new Railyard District.

The menu features elevated bar selections. Some fan favorites include poblano nachos, chipotle chicken, and Cuban pork sandwiches. The blackened tuna salad is often ordered for lunch. As for cocktails, electric lemonade and mermaid water are popular. While some items are standards, updated menus are available on location.

Gatherings are emphasized. Trivia nights, bingo, and dart leagues draw crowds while Taco Tuesdays include creative combinations and gift card raffles. Aside from Husker game days or when Pinnacle Bank arena has events, happy hour specials and other specials are available.

300 Canopy St., No. 140
(402) 261-4140
gate25lnk.com

OTHER LOCAL SPORTS BARS

Brewskys
Haymarket: 201 N. 8th St.
Phone: (402) 328-2739
North: 2662 Cornhusker Hwy.
Phone: (402) 466-2739
South: 1602 South St.
Phone: (402) 438-2739
East: 2840 S. 70th St.
Phone: (402) 483-2739
brewskys.com

Cappy's Hot Spot Bar and Grill
5560 S. 48th St.
(402) 421-1424
cappysbar.com

The Garage Sports Bar/Grill
5551 S. 48th St.
(402) 423-2996
garagebarand
grilllincoln.com

The N Zone Sports Bar & Grill
728 Q St.
(402) 475-8683
facebook.com/thenzonebar

Press Box Sports Bar & Grille
5601 S. 56th St.
(402) 261-3859
pressboxlincoln.com

Risky's Sports Bar and Grill
4680 Leighton Ave.
(402) 466-6966
riskysbar.com

Rosie's Sports Bar
1501 Center Park Rd.
(402) 420-6262
rosiessportsbar.com

Spikes Beach Bar and Grill
2300 Judson St.
(402) 477-1175
spikesbbg.com

Sportscasters Bar and Grill
(also offers a gluten free menu)
3048 N. 70th St.
(402) 466-6679
sportscasterslincoln.com

SOMETHING FOR EVERYONE
AT GOLDENROD PASTRIES

Angela Garbacz needed a creative outlet. After switching to dairy-free eating, she started her "Goldenrod Pastries" blog to share experiments with a new style of baking. Readers began to contact her with requests to buy her creations and after one year of baking from home, she opened her popular storefront bakery in 2015.

Goldenrod Pastries is an inclusive bakery. In addition to dairy-free treats, the bakery offers gluten-free and vegan treats. The bakery caters to as many dietary restrictions as possible. Nut allergies are more complicated, but if this woman-powered bakery has enough notice, accommodations will be made.

Angela's baking approach has led her to being featured in numerous magazines. Her first cookbook, *Perfectly Golden,* shares many recipes, including her most requested one, crumble-buns. She is changing the pastry world, one sprinkle at a time.

3947 S. 48th St.
(402) 486-4103
goldenrodpastries.com

OTHER LOCAL DESSERT OPTIONS

Butterfly Bakery
4209 S. 33rd St.
(402) 475-0620
butterflybakeryne.com

Cookie Company
(Two locations)
138 N. 12th St.
(402) 475-0625
Gateway Mall
61st & O.
(402) 466-7294
thecookieco.com

Cupcakes & More
5700 Old Cheney Rd.
Ste. 2
(402) 261-6214
cupcakesandmore
lincoln.com

**Gratitude Café
and Bakery**
1551 N. Cotner Blvd.
gratitudecafebakery.com

High Society Cheesecake
5600 S. 48th St., Ste. 120
(402) 328-2343
highsociety
cheesecake.com

Misky Bakery
505 N. 27th St., No. 8
(402) 742-0017
facebook.com/
miskybakeryusa

The Rabbit Hole Bakery
800 Q St., Ste. 10
(402) 975-2322
TheRabbitHole
Bakery.com

The Warm Cookie
3700 S. Ninth St. A
(402) 310-2881
thewarmcookie.com

DINE
DOWN HAVELOCK AVENUE

Back in 1995, the former Havelock Fire Station became a café. Displayed throughout the restaurant are historic firefighting artifacts. Classic breakfast items include omelets, pancakes, sandwiches, and soups. Great service is provided at reasonable prices.

Engine House Café
6028 Havelock Ave.
(402) 467-2880, enginehousecafe.com

What began as a "bottle club" expanded to include an outdoor grill. Soon an official restaurant opened and was named Misty's for the owners' favorite song. The original owners filled barrels and then rolled them down an alley to blend their special seasonings, which are still sold today. Misty's has earned Best Prime Rib and Best Steak awards.

6235 Havelock, (402) 466-8424
200 N. 11th St., (402) 476-7766
mistyslincoln.com

Misty's bartender Dave Cole took over a secondary restaurant space in 1984. Lunch specials are available to go. A large reception hall hosts many events. Be sure to order the specialty, the "Leaning Tower of Pizza," which is topped with pepperoni, hamburger, pepperoncinis, onion, and a perfected original sauce on a thinner crust.

6232 Havelock Ave.
(402) 464-1858, islespubandpizza.com

SCREAM OUT
IVANNA CONE

Amy Green loves ice cream. Since 1997, she has devoted her life's work to taking her Ivanna Cone ice cream to the next level. About 17 flavors are featured daily. Standard on the menu are chocolate, vanilla, ice milk, a sherbet, and dairy-free sorbet. Flavors reflect local happenings and include such fun flavors as coffee, chocolate krispie, grape soda, strawberry balsamic peppercorn, and passion fruit sherbet. Waffle cones are also made fresh.

Two important steps provide the best flavor: Ice creams are slow churned in barrel freezers for several hours and the fresh ice cream is flash-frozen to seal the flavor inside.

Being a part of the community matters to Ivanna Cone. Proceeds from particular flavors go to local charitable organizations. Before indulging, plan ahead because only cash and checks are accepted.

701 P St.
(402) 477-7473
ivannacone.com

TIP
If you want to try other creative homemade ice cream flavors, both the two (402) Creamery locations (402creamery.com) and the UNL Dairy Store (dairystore.unl.edu) also change their menus often.

BITE A BIG BURGER
AT HONEST ABE'S

Erik Hustad's friends liked his kitchen experiments and soon he realized his cooking hobby had career potential. After attending a culinary school in Seattle, Erik and his wife returned home to gain restaurant experience. This led to a food truck that Erik started with his cousin, Gabe Lovelace. Their GUP (GroundUp) Kitchen served sandwiches and soon they leased a kitchen to help with food prep. To afford the place, they started serving "Honest Abe's Burgers and Freedom" and within weeks they were selling out every day.

"Honest Abe's" locally sourced beef, flavor combinations, and Parmesan truffle fries caught the public's eye. GUP was gone, and Abe's became the focus. Tripadvisor declared they had the third-best burger in America.

Today five classic burgers are served at all four locations. One, named "1809" for Lincoln's birth year, includes pickled apples, smoked gouda, sweet smoky mayo, and bacon. Four rotating seasonal burgers and a weekly burger vary at each location. There are more than 100 possibilities, so customers can discover many favorites.

GROUNDUP RESTAURANTS

Honest Abe's
840 N. 70th St.
(402) 261-9860

126 N. 14th St.
(402) 261-4904

2662 Cornhusker Highway, Ste. 9
(402) 975-2424

8340 Glynoaks Dr.
(531) 500-5970
grounduprestaurants.com

THE GROUNDUP RESTAURANT TAPAS RESTAURANT AND BAR

Sebastian's Table/Eleanora Bar
8340 Glynoaks Dr., Ste. 100
(531) 500-5402, sebastianstable.com

Other Local Burger Places

HF Crave
4800 Holdrege St., Ste. 100
(402) 480-7399, Hfcrave.com

Nitro Burger
2050 Cornhusker Hwy.
(402) 570-6433, nitroburgerbomb.com

TAKE A SIP
AT JAMES ARTHUR VINEYARDS

What started in 1997 as a hobby of producing wine quickly became more for James Arthur and Neenie Jeffers, along with their daughter Barb and son-in-law Jim Ballard. Now three generations are involved in the state's largest and oldest winery operation. Their farm winery includes 20 acres. To add contrast to their wine selections, they also buy grapes from other Nebraska growers.

Every step of the process (growing, pruning, picking, fermenting, and bottling), happens at James Arthur Vineyards and many wines and ciders are available. Edelweiss, a semi-sweet white wine, is a favorite. Guests can sample wines for a nominal fee at the Winery. Nebraska-produced cheese and bread baskets can also be purchased. Down in the Haymarket, the "From Nebraska" shop offers tastings as well.

> 2001 W. Raymond Rd
> Raymond, NE 68428
> (402) 783-5255
> jamesarthurvineyards.com

TIP

Surrounding Lincoln are additional local wineries. Please look up Deer Springs Winery near Waverly (deerspringswinery.com), Capitol View Winery & Vineyard near Roca (capitolviewwinery.com), Junto Wino near Seward (juntowine.com) and WindCrest Winery (windcrestwinery.com) for more information.

EXCITE YOUR TASTE BUDS
AT THE OVEN

When Ngawang Richen immigrated from India, his first job was working in a New York restaurant. About a decade later, he relocated to the Midwest to become the Oven's head chef. Soon he took over ownership.

Northern Indian cuisine is served with an emphasis placed on using deep colors and intense flavors. Meats marinate for hours. Because peppers are in several dishes, those with sensitive palates should ask for recommendations. By cooking primarily in a Tandoor-style oven, unique flavors abound. Naan bread is prepared fresh daily.

Not only does the Oven serve up delicious food, but it offers quality service in an authentic atmosphere. Its vast wine cellar, which includes over 1,800 selections, has gained recent attention as well. The restaurant was awarded the 2019 Wine Spectators Award.

201 N. 8th St.
(402) 475-6118
101 Pioneer Woods Dr., No. 110
(402) 488-0650
theoven-lincoln.com

TIP
Indian Cuisine varies by region. Two additional Lincoln locations, Aroma Indian Cuisine (aromaindiancusine.com) and Tandoor (tandoor-lincoln.com) have different menu offerings.

RELISH YOUR EXPERIENCE
AT LAZLO'S BREWERY AND GRILL

As Nebraska's first brewpub, Lazlo's has set the standard high. Serving excellent food and drink is expected. Lazlo's Laws are 10 guidelines that emphasize exceptional customer service. Success is attributed to guests having a cozy, comfortable, and positive experience. Fireplaces add ambience and outdoor patio seating offers options.

Many menu items are prepared over a hickory wood grill and the tantalizing aroma draws in customers. The French dip sandwich is a specialty, seafood is flown in daily, and burgers are made fresh. Homemade soups simmer on the stove all day.

Because of the direct connection to Empyrean Brewing Company, guests can also sample new beers on cask nights. The Watchman IPA is brewed with Nebraska hops, and the Dark Side vanilla porter is also popular. Monthly tours of the brewery are provided.

Historic Haymarket
210 N. Seventh St.
(402) 434-5636

5900 Old Cheney Road
(402) 323-8500
lazlosbreweryandgrill.com

Fireworks Restaurant
(also owned/operated by Telesis)
5750 S. 86th Dr.
(402) 434-5644
fireworksrestaurant.com

SIMILAR RESTAURANTS WITH FULL MENUS AND DRINK OPTIONS

Carmelo's Bistro and Wine Bar
4141 Pioneer Woods Dr.
(402) 489-0005
carmelasbistroand
winebar.com

Dino's
2901 S. 84th St., No. 16
(402) 327-0200
dinoslincoln.com

Grata Bar and Lounge
6891 A Street, Ste. 108
(402) 261-3019
gratabar.com

JTK Cuisine and Cocktails
201 N. Seventh St., No. 107
(402) 435-0161
jtkrestaurant.com

9 South Char Grill
844 South St.
(402) 474-9997
9southgrill.com

The Single Barrel
130 N. 10th
(402) 904-4631
thesinglebarrel.com

Stur 22 Lounge
(Caribbean and African Kitchen)
2110 Winthrop Rd.
(402) 805-4579
stur22lounge.com
(events for adults)

SAVOR A SLICE
AT LAZZARI'S PIZZA

New York-style pizza can be found in Lincoln. Since 1993, Lazzari's has been using fresh ingredients to create its specialties. In the store, meats are sautéed, cheese is shredded, and sauces are homemade. This restaurant started downtown and served many lunches, as well as the after-hour bar crowd but, over time, Lincoln's atmosphere changed. Lazzari's added another pizza place in the suburbs. Now this is the only location.

Several creative combinations are available. One of the signature slices honors a frequent customer. "The Randy Ross" features spicy chicken, pepperoni, and cream cheese. Creating unique pizzas such as Bull's Eye barbecue, taco special, crab Rangoon, and baked potato pizzas makes this Lincoln original stand apart.

The local owners want their restaurant to be approachable. Families are welcome. The restaurant also often supports community outreach organizations.

4701 Old Cheney Rd.
(402) 423-0234
lazzarispizza.com

ADDITIONAL LOCAL PIZZERIAS

Big Sal's Pizza and Wings
838 N. 27th St.
(402) 474-7832
bigsalspizza.com

daVinci's
4344 O St.
4120 S. 48th
745 S. 11th
2650 Superior St.
2901 Pine Lake Rd., Ste. G
(402) 475-1111
davincis.com

Huskerville Pub and Pizza
2805 NW 48th St.
(402) 261-9895
facebook.com/
HuskervillePub

MoMo's Pizzeria and Ristorante
7701 Pioneers Blvd.
(402) 261-5966
momo-pizzeria.com

Piezano's
2740 South St.
(402) 474-3355
mypiezanos.com

Ramos Pizza/Buster's BBQ and Grill
2435 S. 48th St.
(402) 483-5050
ramosandbusters.com

Yia Yia's
yiayiaspizzaandbeer.com
1423 O St.
(402) 477-9166
OR 2840 S. 70th St., Ste. 5
(531) 500-4937
yiayiaspizzaandbeer.com

NIBBLE ON A CROISSANT
AT LE QUARTIER BAKERY

Before moving from Montreal to live near his brother, John Quiring experimented with home baking in Seattle. Living near a French bakery inspired John to pursue culinary training at a local school and later in Paris.

In 2006, John moved back to his home state of Nebraska to start his Lincoln Le Quartier Bakery. His brother, Seth, soon joined him. They wanted a "Q" in the bakery name. Since Quartier means neighborhood, this reflects their goal to create local baked goods that all can enjoy.

The bread case is filled with over a dozen delicious possibilities. Nine pastries are standard offerings, along with other desserts. Those on vegan and gluten-free diets can discuss options. The café offers homemade soups and sandwiches, including a popular chicken salad croissant.

6900 "O" St., Ste. 132
(402) 464-0345
lequartierbakingco.com

OTHER RESTAURANTS WITH FRENCH OFFERINGS

Normandy
2785 S. 17th St.
(402) 476-0606
thenormandylnk.com

Green Gateau
330 S. 10th St.
(402) 477-0330
greengateau.com

ANOTHER TYPE OF BREAD BAKERY

Bagels & Joe
4701 Old Cheney Rd.
7811 Pioneers Blvd., Ste. 101
1777 N. 86th St., Ste. 104
(402) 423-7797 (Same phone number for all)
bagelsandjoe.com

STAY CAFFEINATED
AT THE MILL

Although the Mill was started in 1978 because the original owners wanted to get great coffee at wholesale prices, this coffee shop now has its own culture. In the early days, Dan Sloan helped with the accounting. Today he and his wife, Tamara, are the sole owners. She added her own flair to the shop by adding a line of specialty teas.

Getting a cup of coffee is meant to be an experience. Baristas are trained to guide the customers in picking a drink that could become a favorite. If the beverage does not satisfy, guests are allowed to return it and try again.

Beans are ethically sourced in areas where farmers are fairly treated. Because the beans are roasted at the Haymarket Mill, guests are assured a fresh cup of coffee. The two newest locations also serve beer and wine, with an emphasis on locally produced beverages.

The Mill Coffee & Tea in the Historic Haymarket (original)
800 P St.
(402) 475-5522, millcoffee.com

The Mill Coffee & Tea at Telegraph
330 S. 21st St.
(402) 327-1991

The Mill Coffee & Bistro at Nebraska Innovation Campus
2021 Transformation Dr.
(402) 413-9191

The Mill Coffee & Tea at College View
4736 Prescott Ave.
(402) 327-9391

OTHER LINCOLN COFFEE HOUSES

The Coffee House
1324 P St., Main Floor
(402) 477-6611
thecoffeehouselnk.com

Harbor Coffeehouse
1265 S. Cotner Blvd
(402) 489-1720
601 P St., Ste. 102
(531) 500-2353
harborcoffeehouse.com

Lincoln Espresso
112 S. 16th St.
facebook.com/
lincolnespresso

Mo Java Café & Roasting Company
2649 N. 48th St., Ste. D
(402) 464-4130
mojava.net

nuVibe (Juice & Java)
Café: 4131 Pioneer
Woods Dr., No. 108
Drive Thru: 5520 Old
Cheney Rd.
(402) 904-7155
nuvibecoffee.com

CELEBRATE LIFE
AT THE PARTHENON GREEK GRILL AND TAVERNA

When the Kazas family immigrated from Greece, they operated several Greek restaurants. In 2002, their sons, George and Mike, followed the family tradition. Their menu is based on their mother's recipes, with some culinary twists. Brandy is used to help the saganaki and kasseri cheese flambé for a popular appetizer. Moussaka, pastitsio, and dolmathes are customer favorites. A dessert case features Greek specialties, including varieties of baklava.

With locally sourced produce, Nebraska-raised lamb and fresh fish arriving weekly, the meals are fresh. During the summer months, guests can dine on the patio. Various annual celebratory nights, such as Greek Independence Day, lead to creative menus. Area musicians and dancers add flavor to festive evenings. Monthly wine specialty dinners often sell out.

5500 S. 56th St., No. 8
(402) 423-2222
theparthenon.net

TIP
For other variations of Mediterranean cuisine, please check out these additional local favorites: Ali Baba Gyros, George's Gourmet Grill Downtown, Habibi Kabob and Schwarama along with Sultan's Kite. For those craving African cuisine, please try the Tiru Ethiopian Restaurant.

EAT
AWARD-WINNING BARBECUE AT PHAT JACK'S

The ability to transform leftover rib pieces into a new dish takes talent. One bite of Phat Jack's signature burnt ends explains why this specialty dish often sells out. Many meats are offered, and the "Psycho" sandwich includes both brisket and pork.

After perfecting their barbecue techniques while living in Kansas City, Lincoln graduates Matt and Jackie Burt came home in 2004 to start Phat Jack's. At a barbecue competition prior to their move, he chose the name that now defines his restaurant. "Pretty hot and tasty" does describe their unique Kansas City-Texas style of barbecue. (The Jack part is a bit more random.)

Matt has won numerous awards for his style of barbecue. One of the appeals of smoking food for Matt is the fact that preferred barbecue techniques are unique to both regions and people. Meat can be purchased by the pound and catering is available.

101 SW 14th Pl.
(402) 464-7428
phatjackslincoln.com

15

WALK TO CENTRALLY LOCATED PIEDMONT BISTRO BY VENUE

Since 1963, this location has served various restaurants. In 2017, the local Pillar Restaurant Group, owners of popular Venue Restaurant and Lounge, purchased the space and rebranded it. Guests enjoy dining in the comfortable setting. For special events, the Cotner Room is available.

Midwestern comfort food is made from locally sourced ingredients. At brunch, build your own eggs Benedict and enjoy a popular pitcher of mimosa. Creative sandwiches, salads, and slowly simmered soups are lunch features. At dinner, order delicious Nebraska beef steaks or daily flow-in seafood. Specialty sides include beet fries and maple-soy glazed Brussels sprouts.

Mixologists serve hand-crafted cocktails using house-made syrups. Patio seating is available and small dogs are even welcome, with canine cuisine being offered.

Due to its central location, many walk or bike to grab a bite. This restaurant is involved in the community and guests and staff are treated like family. Exceptional citizens are recognized through the "Piedmont Heroes" program. Piedmont truly is your "friendly neighborhood bistro located on the corner of Cotner and A."

1265 S. Cotner Blvd., Ste. 38
(402) 975-2816
piedmontbistro.com

OTHER PILLAR RESTAURANT LOCATIONS

Venue Restaurant and Lounge
4111 Pioneer Woods Dr., Ste. 100
(402) 488-8368
Yourvenue.net

Cactus: Modern Mexican & Catina
5500 S. 56th St., Ste. 1
(531) 500-4444
cactusmmc.com

OTHER LINCOLN AMERICANA ORIGINALS

Billy's Restaurant
1308 H St.
(402) 474-0084
billysrestaurant.com

Dish Restaurant
1100 O St.
(402) 475-9575
dishdowntown.com

M & J's Southern Style Food
333 Cotner Blvd., No. 1
(402) 304-4810

SLOW DOWN DINNER
AT PRAIRIE PLATE

When the Cornett family was stationed at Offut Air Force Base in Bellevue, Nebraska, the experience changed their lives. As a naval aviator, Jerry enjoyed the slower Midwest pace. His wife Renee, a retired Navy ensign who served as a helicopter pilot, used that posting to gain a culinary degree. Continued travel influenced her approach both to cooking and to life.

Upon Jerry's retirement, the Cornetts relocated to Nebraska and began Lakehouse Farm. They started growing certified organic fruits and vegetables for farmers' markets in 2012. Two years later, Prairie Plate Restaurant, based on a farm-to-table philosophy, opened in the middle of their farmland.

From April to December, restaurant hours are predictable and a few scheduled winter special events are offered. Menus are based upon the produce that is available. Slow food is emphasized and plates are sure to be fresh, delicious, and good for you.

10405 Branched Oak Rd.
Waverly, NE 68462
(402) 786-2239, prairieplaterestaurant.com

TIP
If you are unable to leave town for the farm, The Hub Café (hubcafelincoln.com) near downtown Lincoln also offers farm-to-table fare.

NOSH
IN THE NEIGHBORHOOD AT TOAST

Northwest Lincoln needed a neighborhood restaurant. Initially, Toast started as a high-quality counter service delicatessen. To provide a cozy and welcoming atmosphere, the restaurant repurposed building materials reclaimed from Lincoln's retired Whittier Junior High, Omaha's former Burlington Railroad Station, and other local buildings.

While the sandwiches and coffee were popular, Toast's loyal customers wanted more, so the owners transformed the store into a full-service, casual dining restaurant focused on updated comfort food. Not surprisingly, the Fallbrook burger is popular, featuring homemade bacon jam, crispy avocado, pickled red onion, fresh arugula, sweet poppy seed mayo, and bleu cheese on a toasted gourmet bun. Fried chicken with smoky gouda sauce is delicious.

Daily lunch break options provide a delicious alternative to fast food. Toast is also proud to be considered the local watering hole, with unique cocktails that change seasonally and a good selection of local breweries on tap. Here's a toast to friendship and community.

570 Fallbrook Blvd., No. 105
(402) 261-8859, Gettoasty.com

TIP

If you enjoy Toast, you will also like the other Red Herring Concepts Restaurant, Lead Belly (getleaded.com), which is located in Lincoln's Haymarket.

TRY
BEEF AND CABBAGE SANDWICHES AT RUNZA

Entrepreneur Sally Everett started selling Runza sandwiches at a southwest Lincoln food stand in 1949. Beef, cabbage, onions, and spices were cooked inside the bread dough. Runza was easy to say and easy to trademark. The original price was 15 cents.

Almost 20 years later, Sally's son, Don, started the first franchise on 56th street. He also sold Runzas out of the back of an old mail truck at Husker games. Now Runzas are available inside the stadium and there are over 80 locations in four states.

Before the drive-thru was established, car hops brought food out to the customers. For a while, Runza played up its German-Russian roots by having servers wear lederhosen. "The food that Grandma used to make" was once the slogan.

In the winter on Temperature Tuesdays, the temperature reading at 6 a.m. dictates the price of an Original Runza Sandwich plus a side order and drink. Food is made fresh daily and includes the restaurant's signature onion rings. Other popular menu items include burgers plus chili, with cinnamon rolls.

14 Lincoln locations	Also Owned by Runza
Longest operating location	Braeda Fresh Express Café
1501 N. 56th St.	4231 S. 33rd St.
(402) 466-1087, runza.com	(402) 488-6767, braeda.com

OTHER LINCOLN AREA FAST FOOD PLACES

Amigos
(402) 488-8500
14 Lincoln locations including 6891 A St.
(402) 488-8500, amigoskings.com

D'Leons
Several Lincoln Locations
Open late (Some are open 24 hour)
Original franchise: 2140 W. O St.
(402) 438-7100

FlyDogz Lincoln
3111 O St.
(402) 475-4059
flydogz.us

Taco Inn
(Try the flour nachos!)
245 S. 70th St., (402) 488-6114
1430 N. 56th St., (402) 466-4970
4039 S. 48th St., (402) 483-1416
2509 N. 11th St., (402) 476-6064
tacoinn.net

ORDER BREAKFAST
(AND PIES) ALL DAY
AT STAUFFER'S CAFÉ & PIE SHOPPE

In 1996, Clarity Stauffer started a café with her son, Thad. She is still the baker and he is the cook. Through the years, multiple family members have worked at the cafe and today seven Stauffers are a part of the family restaurant.

Breakfast is offered all day. Rotating specials keep the menu interesting and guests come back weekly for the liver and onions. The café offers classics that are more difficult to find today. On football Saturdays in the fall, the Big Red open-faced chili burger can be ordered.

Over 50 pies are on the menu and about 35 flavors are available daily. Sour cream raisin and lemon meringue seem to be crowd favorites. If customers want a certain kind of pie, they can call a few days ahead to request a specific flavor. Cookies and muffins are often available. Custom cakes are also available by special order.

5600 S. 48th St.
(402) 423-2206
staufferscafe.com

OTHER LINCOLN ORIGINALS WHERE BREAKFAST IS SERVED ALL DAY

The Doughnut Hole
5600 S. 48th St.
(402) 413-7516

Eatery
2548 S. 48th St.
(402) 489-0396
theeateryrestaurant.com

Good Evans
6891 A St., Ste. 102
(402) 488-3444
goodevans.com

Greenfield's Restaurant
7900 S. 87th St.
(402) 420-3232
greenfieldscafe.com

Penelope's Lil' Café
4724 Pioneers Blvd.
(402) 435-0998
facebook.com/
penelopeslincoln

Randy's Donuts
201 Capitol Beach Blvd., Ste. 5
(402) 435-7992

Virginia's Travelers Café
3820 Cornhusker Hwy.
(402) 464-9885

CHOMP ON
COMPLIMENTARY CHIPS AND SALSA AT TICO'S RESTAURANT AND TEQUILA BAR

Tico's is known for its seasoned chips, chile rellenos, and chicken and cream enchiladas. Unique Ticorittos are filled with rice, beans, and beef, then topped with a chile sauce. Featuring ice cream, sopapillas, and wine sauce, the ponsonita sundae is a dessert specialty.

Thursday night's happy hour special may feature the best specialty of the week. Tico's famous margaritas are the drink special. Now the restaurant also features tequila house infusions and flights.

The Loft provides a rare downtown meeting space where patrons can choose to serve a Mexican buffet. Businesses often use the room at lunch and many birthdays and engagements have been celebrated here.

317 S. 17th St.
(402) 475-1048
ticosoflincoln.com

MORE LOCAL MEXICAN RESTAURANTS

Copal Progressive Mexican Cuisine
4747 Pioneers Blvd.
(402) 486-0488

El Chaparro
900 S. 13th St.
(402) 435-7112

El Rancho
2700 "O" St.
(402) 476-2800

Hacienda Real
3130 Pine Lake Rd.
(402) 423-0525

Hacienda Real Highlands
4811 NW First St., No. 101
(402) 476-0654

La Paloma
8320 Northwoods Dr.
(402) 489-3683

La Paz
321 N. Cotner Blvd.
(402) 466-9111

El Toro
2600 S. 48th St., Ste. 17
(402) 488-3939

Las Margaritas
2700 Jamie Lane
(402) 421-2662

Mazatlan
211 N. 70th
(402) 464-7201

Mazatlan II
2701 King Ln.
(402) 438-0665

Pancho Villa Mexican Grill
5800 Cornhusker Hwy., Ste. 10
(402) 466-7818

Super Taco
5501 Holdrege St., Ste. D
(402) 465-8505

Taqueria El Rey
116 S. 27th St.
(402) 742-5367

TASTE THE TRADITION
AT VALENTINO'S

This Lincoln ristorante has lived out its definition that "food restores" since 1957. Val and Zena Weiller opened an Italian pizzeria at their former fruit market location. Starting with three dozen pizza pans and family recipes, this University of Nebraska East Campus location was so popular that patrons were willing to wait an hour for a table.

Around 1972, the Messineo and Alesio families took over and expanded the concept. Now Valentino's has 35 restaurants in four states. "The Old Pizza Chef" logo is often featured as a reminder that its classic approach matters. One distinction of Valentino's is its daily simmered sauce.

While a decadent buffet is offered, this simple meal is still one owner's favorite: A slice of hamburger pizza, a salad with homemade creamy Italian dressing, and a Romano cheese roll. This classic combination is tasting tradition at its best.

3535 Holdrege St.
(402) 467-3611

2701 S. 70th St.
(402) 437-9177

2820 Pine Lake Rd.
(402) 420-6800

Ten additional "To-go" locations are available
Valentinos.com

ADDITIONAL LINCOLN CLASSICS (ALL OVER 30 YEARS OLD)

Billy's Restaurant
1301 H St.
(402) 474-0084
billysrestaurant.com

Lee's Chicken
1940 W. Van Dorn St.
(402) 477-4339
leeschickenlincoln.com

Tina's Café and Catering
616 South St.
(402) 435-9404
tinascafelincoln.com

ELEVATE YOUR EXPECTATIONS
AT ZIPLINE BREWING CO.

Longtime friends James Gallentine and Tom Wilmouth wanted to start a brewery. A chance meeting with Marcus Powers over softball resulted in a collaborative effort to market local ales. James's son inspired the brewery's name. After he crashed and burned on an unfinished backyard zipline the men were inspired. Even with the unknowns, they would move forward with the adventure.

Three hundred test batches led to these initial beers: Cooper Alt, Oatmeal Porter, and a NZ IPA. Still today, new flavors are tested in micro-batches. Offerings continue to expand and some are sold in bottles. Many more beers are available through tap rooms and local bars. Seasonal beers, such as milk stout, are offered until the barrels run dry.

Zipline's commitment to the community helps it stand out. It has collaborated with other breweries and sold specialty beers to fund conservation efforts. Through recycling and repurposing, the brewery has achieved a zero waste designation.

2100 Magnum Cir., Ste. 1
(402) 475-1001

5168 Brewing
5730 Hidcote Dr.
(402) 875-5588

Beer Hall
5740 Hidcote Dr., Ste. B

https://ziplinebrewing.com/
Note: The above addresses are all related to Zipline Locations

ADDITIONAL LOCAL BREWERIES

Backswing Brewing Co.
500 W. South St., No. 8
(402) 413-5576, backswingbrewing.com

Boiler Brewing Company
129 N. 10th St., No. 8
(402) 261-8775, boilerbrewingcompany.com

Code Beer Company
200 S. Antelope Valley Pkwy.
(402) 318-5888, codebeer.com

Cosmic Eye Brewing
6800 P St., No. 300
(531) 500-2739, cosmiceye.beer

Empyrean Brewing Co.
729 Q St., (402) 434-5960
empyreanbrewingco.com

White Elm Brewing Co.
720 Van Dorn St.
(402) 261-6078, whiteelmbrewing.com

ARTS AND ENTERTAINMENT

SING ALONG
AT ABENDMUSIK AT FIRST-PLYMOUTH

In 1972, the First-Plymouth Church artistic director determined his congregation needed more musical opportunities. Initially, only church members participated in this choral program, but a nonprofit organization was formed in 1981. Community members joined.

Nearly 100 singers perform for Abendmusik today. Musicians with an interest in choral music can try out. Singers must be devoted to choral music. There are multiple concerts throughout the year, and nationally known musicians sometimes participate.

Youth Masterworks became a part of the program to provide local high schools with the opportunity to have a high-caliber experience. Chosen schools practice their music throughout the year and then perform under a guest conductor.

Some concerts charge admission but many are free. The artistic director plans the season's music and guest artists. The executive director and administrator work together on the details.

2000 D St.
(402) 476-9933, abendmusik.org

TIP
On many Sunday mornings, their 57 bells peal to announce services. First-Plymouth has one of only two carillon towers in Nebraska. A console is played from the tower.

SEE A LIVE SHOW
AT BOURBON THEATRE

Transforming the former State Theater into a small concert venue was an inspired idea. Because the floor is already sloped, patrons can see the stage from various angles. For smaller performances, a simpler setup with less seating is also available.

Seating is assigned for some shows, but most are general admission, which implies a standing-room-only situation. A limited number of tickets are sold, but concert-goers may want to arrive earlier for those events. This location has proven to be the launching pad for many artists getting started in the music business. Shows often sell out and certain performances are only for the 18-or 21-and-up crowds.

Having a drink at the bar is a part of the experience. House-made pomegranate grenadine, ginger syrup, and sweet and sour mix add a splash of interest to custom cocktails. To order alcoholic versions, a valid ID is required.

1405 O St.
Bourbontheatre.com

TIP
If the Bourbon Theater is not having an event, the Rococco Theater (rococotheatre.com) and Royal Grove (rhproyal18.wpenguine.com) also often have live musical performances.

SMILE,
YOU'RE AT CHAMPIONS FUN CENTER

Champions Fun Center sells smiles. Since 1996, it has been in the business of providing a safe place for kids, especially tweens, to enjoy themselves. With dozens of arcade games, a giant maze, and cosmic bowling, even the weather can't stop the fun. On warmer days, miniature golf, go-karts, batting cages, and water wars are additional attractions. The four-story free fall is another option for those up for a thrill. Patrons can pay per attraction, but all-day passes, wristbands, and family specials offer deals.

Victory Lane features carnival food, including a local pizza favorite, DaVinci's. The family owned pizza restaurant has operated Champions since 2000. This venue is a great place for birthday parties as several packages are available and include both attraction options and pizza. After visiting Champions, guests agree that there is so much fun and so much to do.

1555 Yolande Ave.
(402) 434-7066
Championsfuncenter.com

> **TIP**
> Across town, Lost in Fun (lostinfun.com) is geared toward younger children.

SOLVE A PUZZLE
AT ESCAPE ROOM LINCOLN

Being stuck in a room may not sound fun at first, but solving a puzzle before time runs out is exciting. Sleuths can pick one of four themed rooms to enter. To keep options interesting, new rooms are rotated into the lineup. While previous themes are not recycled, particular props are used again.

Room development inspiration comes from various places, including books, television, and movies. With time and experience, more immersive rooms are created. The Escape Lincoln team enjoys introducing new techniques and technology to keep the experience entertaining.

Having customers return to try another puzzle is the best part. Customizing the experience is part of the fun, especially when a marriage proposal is involved. Abby Bartholomew, co-creator of Escape Lincoln, emphasizes that "we enjoy getting to be a part of their stories."

815 O St., Ste. 2
(531) 500-4475
escapelincoln.com

> **TIP**
> There is additional nearby entertainment. Tomahawks Ax Throwing is located in the same building. Down the street, the Lincoln Escape Room opened up about the same time and offers additional entertainment.

JAZZ IN JUNE

Young art lovers wanted a way to connect Lincoln citizens to the Sheldon Museum of Art sculpture garden. About 500 people came to the first Jazz in June in 1992. Initially, local and university musicians played at the four Tuesday June concerts. Now performers are from international stages and have included Grammy award-winning artists such as Arturo Sandoval and Terrence Blanchard.

Today 4,000 to 5,000 people attend each outdoor concert. Besides music, attendees may also enjoy the market, which features a variety of food trucks and wares created by local artisans. While the backdrop is still the Sheldon Sculpture Gardens, the next-door Lied Center is now curating the concerts and performers. Recently, it also began offering jazz camps for kids in cooperation with the Lincoln Children's Museum.

12th and R Sheldon Sculpture Garden and Green Space
Jazzinjune.com

FOLLOW THE LIED CENTER

Watching "Madame Butterfly" at the first Lied Center event in 1990 was a dream come true for many. For decades, Lincoln locals had been longing for a venue to host grand-scale events. Other locations were either too small or unsuitable for majestic performances. Ernst Lied had graduated from the University of Nebraska in 1927. Executrix Christine Hinson earmarked Lied Foundation Trust funds to start the process.

Between the floor seating and the balconies, 2,258 guests can enjoy main stage performances. The Johnny Carson Room is a black box theater that features 250 tiered seats. With its perfect acoustics, Kimball Recital Hall next door offers another 850 seats. At these three performance halls, many events happen annually.

Education is another component of the Lied Center. The Lied facilitates onsite workshops and other events throughout the state. Promoting arts across Nebraska is part of its mission.

301 N. 12th St.
(402) 474-4747
Liedcenter.org

PLAY LIKE A KID
AT THE LINCOLN CHILDREN'S MUSEUM

Hands-on learning is essential. Area parents and educators demonstrated this at the August 1988 "Sights and Sounds" event for 10,000 Nebraska State Fair attendees. A year later, the Lincoln Children's Museum opened. Over time, exhibits have been updated and expanded. Yet the museum's mission remains the same—it adheres to the power of play.

Over 40 exhibits provide purposeful fun. Cuckoo Construction expands all three floors, allowing kids to climb and build with foam bricks. Tiny Town is supported by local businesses that have set up pretend shops for kids, including a music shop, a veterinarian, and an orchard. Planes, trains, and astronauts encourage imaginary travel.

As an inclusive community, the museum encourages all visitors. Sensory Night turns down the lights and more for those who cannot handle excessive noise. Before Shining Star Nights, the museum is thoroughly cleaned from top to bottom. This allows kids with immune system deficiencies to play safely. The LPS Family Literacy Night reaches out to the immigrant community and to those whose first language is not English.

1420 P St.
(402) 477-4000
lincolnchildrensmuseum.org

FEED THE GOATS
AT THE LINCOLN CHILDREN'S ZOO

Lincoln already had places to see animals. But in 1965, the Folsom's Children's Zoo opened as a place designed with children in mind. The ZO&O Railroad has always been a part of the fun. In 2019, 345,915 guests visited, making it the second-largest cultural attraction in the state.

The creature selection has changed and grown through the years. Over 400 animals call Lincoln home, with nearly 40 of those on the endangered list. Recent upgrades include the giraffe pavilion. In the spring, guests can watch cheetahs sprint full speed ahead on their own specially designed runs. Two Sumatran Tigers are other recent arrivals.

The zoo's focus also includes conservation. Camps for all ages teach kids to care for animals. Local public school students continue that tradition by attending zoo school. Recently, the zoo transitioned to be open year-round. "Boo at the Zoo" and "Zoo Lights Powered by LES" are popular seasonal offerings.

> 1222 S. 27th St.
> (402) 475-6741
> lincolnzoo.org

TAKE IN LOCAL THEATER
AT THE LINCOLN COMMUNITY PLAYHOUSE

Five performers and six crew members participated in the Lincoln Community Playhouse's inaugural circlet theater, *Springtime for Henry*. This July 1946 production happened at the Lindell Hotel. A complete history of all of playhouse performances and contributors is available online.

The theater is accessible for all performers. Senior citizens can become "Radio Active Players." The Penguin Project pairs special needs artists with peer mentors. Behind-the-scenes assistance is needed with the set.

To make productions affordable, the theater relies on volunteers. Costumes must be sewn and ushers are needed. Only guest directors, choreographers, and stage directors are paid positions. The goal is to provide the finest quality theater experience in both process and production.

2500 S. 56th St.
(402) 489-7529, Lincolnplayhouse.com

TIP
If you are interested in seeing more theater, there are several additional places that offer local productions.
Haymarket Theatre (haymarkettheatre.org)
The Stage Theater in Hickman (thestagetheater.com)
TADA Theater (tadaproductions.info)
Theatre Arts for Kids (tafk.org)

LISTEN CLOSELY
TO LINCOLN'S SYMPHONY ORCHESTRA

In 1927, a group of Lincoln musicians wanted to enrich the lives of local children by providing musical exposure and teaching event etiquette. Back then, performances took place in a local church, but today concerts are performed at the Lied Center. Guest artists, including Aaron Copland, Ray Charles, Tony Bennett, and Ben Folds, have joined the locals.

Today the symphony performs 10 concerts per year. Two are family shows with discounted ticket prices. In addition, the LSO presents Young People's Concerts each spring. These shows provide older elementary students with the opportunity to hear familiar pieces in a grand setting.

Beyond formal performances, symphony members reach out to the community. The "Harmony in Healing" program sends musicians to play music at local hospitals and rehabilitation facilities. Through the "Social Impact Program," tickets are provided to low-income individuals and families.

(402) 476-2211
lincolnsymphony.com

TIP
Offered through Lincoln Public Schools, the Lincoln Youth Symphony allows young people to be a part of an orchestra. Please visit lincolnyouthsymphony.org for more details.

PAINT
YOURSELF SILLY

Encouraging others to create meaningful art that lasts is why Paint Yourself Silly started in 2000. Guests pick out a pottery piece from a wide selection of possibilities and then decorate their selection. About a week later, the completed fired piece is ready. Glass fusing and clay sculpting provide additional art production opportunities.

Group experiences are encouraged. Preschoolers can attend paint and story times. After-school art clubs are student options. Gatherings for adults allow them to rediscover creativity.

Paint Yourself Silly sees art as an important type of communication. Pottery is accessible. Patrons can also preserve a snapshot in time where creations become memorial objects that provide a way to remember and honor family and friends. Since the pieces are functional, this type of art becomes a useful necessity.

4101 Pioneer Woods Dr., Ste. 106
(402) 486-1010

1501 Pine Lake Rd., Ste. 24
(402) 423-1030

paintyourselfsilly.net

SEE A SHOW
AT PINEWOOD BOWL

Surrounded by evergreens, guests have been enjoying events at Pinewood Bowl since 1947. This outdoor theater area honors those brave men and women who fought in World War II. Pioneers Park developers had to wait nearly 20 years for construction to be funded.

Today, up to 5,500 people can attend family shows and local theatrical and musical productions. Without any formal seating, certain performances are for standing-room-only crowds. For other shows, guests can use picnic blankets. Consult the venue website for a list of items not allowed inside.

In the 1990s, concert headliners began appearing. This smaller venue appeals to artists. Through the years, performers have included Willie Nelson, B. B. King, ZZ Top, Ringo Starr, and Steve Martin and Martin Short. Guests can experience "world class concerts under the stars."

3201 S. Coddington Ave.
(402) 904-4444
pinewoodbowltheater.com

TIP
During the summer, the Lincoln Municipal Band offers free outdoor concerts at the Antelope Park John Shildneck Memorial Bandshell.

BE A SPECTATOR
AT PINNACLE BANK ARENA

Not only did the Pinnacle Bank Arena (PBA) change Lincoln's skyline in 2013, but having a bigger venue enhanced Lincoln's opportunities. Bigger musical acts and conferences that had passed on coming to the capital city now were interested. Restaurants, businesses, and apartments moved into the surrounding Railyard District.

All Husker men's and women's basketball games happen in the Vault—the PBA courts nickname. Graduation ceremonies happen here as well. Although some were skeptical at the beginning, PBA is a Lincoln drawing card.

The large-scale artwork near the entrance is titled "Candy Box." This chosen theme is a reminder that Lincoln's second-biggest industry was once confectionery. Artist Donald Lipinski put a lot of meaning into the 144 varied chocolate pieces. Represented are corn, "The Sower," trains, graduation, basketball, Omaha (the big O), and boots that represent hard-working Nebraskans.

400 Pinnacle Arena Dr.
(402) 904-4444
pinnaclebankarena.com

TWIRL AROUND
AT THE PLA MOR BALLROOM

For over 90 years, locals have been dancing the night away at the Pla Mor. Bobby Layne & his Orchestra purchased the ballroom in 1972. After a year of updates, they reopened. Through the years, many bigtime performers such as Lawrence Welk, the Tommy Dorsey Band, and Count Basie and his orchestra have been featured at this venue.

Live country music is featured Sunday nights. Are your boots a bit dusty? Free country line dance lessons are included as a part of the admission price.

On Thursday nights, swing around as a part of Big Band Night. Always wanted to learn how to fox trot, jitterbug, or swing? Ballroom lessons are available. Admission passes are included as part of the price, so learners can practice their steps.

The ballroom provides an elegant atmosphere for wedding receptions, special events, and even fundraisers. Bartending services are included and clients can choose their own caterer.

6600 West O St.
(402) 475-4030
plamorballroom.com

TIP
If you are looking for ballroom dancing exclusively, check out the DelRay Ballroom (thedelray.com).

CELEBRATE FALL
AT ROCA BERRY FARM

Roca Berry Farm was originally used primarily to grow berries and pumpkins. Starting in 1980, guests came out to pick the produce. But growing strawberries in Nebraska is unpredictable and farm operators noticed that kids enjoyed the hayrack rides. Over time, they added more activities and the farm became a fall destination.

Take a ride on the Rocamotive Railway to see the farm layout. From the corn corral and maze to the Dino Dig, kids will be entertained. Go off to the races using prairie dogs or ducks. Play life-size Candyland or jump into a hay bale. During the weekends, try out the barrel coaster and see the cannon ball shoot. These are just a few of the daytime options.

At night, Roca Scary Farm is for the older crowd. With haunted hayrides and a psychopath and sinister circus, the place becomes a bit more frightening at night. Zombie shoots occur on the weekends.

The farm also has two beautifully updated barns that can be leased for events and weddings.

16531 S. 38th St.
Roca, NE 68430
(402) 421-2933, rocaberryfarm.com

TIP
Near Roca Berry Farm is another farm that provides summer family fun. Jeff and Trisha Keiser operate Camp Sonshine out at her family's former farm. Go to campsonshinememories.org to check it out.

BECOME A FILM CRITIC
AT MARY RIEPMA ROSS MEDIA ARTS CENTER

When the Sheldon Museum of Art opened, noteworthy films were a part of its fine art offerings. Independent films and documentaries were featured. While the auditorium was suitable for a time, the need for a separate theater became evident.

Former Lincoln resident Mary Riepma Ross later became a New York City lawyer. Although she never lived in Nebraska again, she continued to be a lifetime supporter of UNL arts. In 1990, she established a trust to help the media center and, 13 years later, the new center was named in her honor. Upon her death in 2013, her will funneled more money into the programs.

With its two theaters, state-of-the-art sound system, and lighting, film studies majors can present their projects. Students learn to critique the arts. Showing films that align outside the mainstream benefits the community. Live performances of the Metropolitan Opera and the London National Theater are also shown on the screens.

313 N. 13th St.
(402) 472-5353, theross.org

> **TIP**
> Another place to see unique films is the historic Joyo Theater (6102 Havelock Ave.). Contact (402) 464-JOYO for more information including how the theater can be rented out for private showings.

SING WITH YOUR SUPPER
AT SCREAMERS DINING AND CABARET

Ray Miller started the Scarlet and Cream Singers as UNL musical ambassadors. Kevin Witcher appreciated the opportunity to grow as a singer. Today he provides local musical novices with a place to grow.

Screamers features "singing servers." Every so often, these local talents sing a few numbers. The styles, eras, and genres of their selections vary. With time for both music and conversation, patrons feel free to come and go. This organic approach provides a relaxing atmosphere.

Tuesday nights are all about kids' music (including many tunes from *Frozen*) and rotating activities that include face painting. During limited lunch hours, tunes reflect the 1950s and 1960s. Discount date nights are also available.

As for audience requests, the motto is, "If we know it, we'll sing it." Sinatra and Elvis top the restaurant charts, along with Ella Fitzgerald's "At Last." Kevin himself is known for his "Unchained Melody" rendition.

By the way, the menu includes everything from steaks to sandwiches. The Brussels sprouts and crab cakes are crowd favorites!

803 Q St., Ste. 150
(531) 500-2550
screamersdining.com

FEEL THE BLUES
AT ZOO BAR

Lining the interior walls of the narrow 1921 brick building are show bills. Hundreds of them. Since 1973, the Zoo Bar has been Lincoln's live music destination. Although artists may be singing the blues, both artists and patrons alike return to hear quality music. Legendary performers have included Buddy Guy, Bo Diddley, Albert Collins, Robert Cray, and Otis Rush.

Live shows happen almost every night. The Zoo Bar opens mid-afternoon and closes after midnight. On nights when performers are not scheduled, the house band plays.

Zoofest has become an annual favorite for many music fans. For two summer nights, musicians take to the streets. In front of the bar, the roads are closed so crowds can enjoy live music. Besides blues shows, performances feature a variety of styles, including funk, rockabilly, and zydeco.

136 N. 14th St.
(402) 435-8754
zoobar.com

SPORTS AND RECREATION

PUTT A HOLE IN ONE
AT ADVENTURE GOLF

When longtime friends Erik Gustafson and Dylan Bohlke took over Adventure Golf, their vision involved far more than having people putting balls. They wanted to create a space where customers can experience joy with those they love. To facilitate community, they have added miniature golf leagues, tournaments, fundraisers, and movie nights. Thanks to their efforts, the Cornhusker State games now include competition at their course. New life has been brought to the 30-year-old course.

Erik points out that being present is a gift and getting away from technology is a plus. Miniature golf provides the opportunity to take a deep breath and relax. Being in a natural setting with the sound of rushing water provides a calming experience. Interrupting the daily routine to have fun allows people to recharge.

5901 S. 56th St.
(402) 421-2254
adventuregolfcenter.com

TRY AN OLLIE
AT THE BAY

Mike Smith decided that kids need three things: a place to be, something to do, and someone who cares about them. By opening The Bay in 2010, he moved toward fulfilling those goals. The first part of his project was opening an indoor skateboard park. For those kids who could not afford the fees, all-access passes were provided.

Now in a permanent location, this nonprofit has expanded its offerings. In the digital arts collective space, kids can learn how to capture/edit photos and videos. Graphic design, illustrations, and coding instruction are also available.

Recently a coffee bar space has been taken over by Goldenrod Pastries. This inclusive bakery offers treats for almost all diets. Concerts are offered on Friday and Saturday nights. The main goal at The Bay is to be a part of the Lincoln community. Everyone is welcome.

2005 Y St.
(402) 310-5215
thebay.org/lincoln

TIP
Two Lincoln parks, Peter Pan Park (32nd and W) and Tierra Briarhurst Park (27th and Tierra) both have outdoor skating ramps.

43

WATCH
CARS GO IN CIRCLES AT EAGLE RACEWAY

Gentlemen, start your Sprint Cars, modifieds, SportMods, Hobby Stocks, and Sport Compacts! At this local raceway, five different IMCA-sanctioned divisions compete during the season. Back in 1963, Dale Halvorson constructed the track on farmland. Ownership has changed hands several times. Since 2007, Roger Hadan has owned and operated the track with his family.

Family fun is promoted. All Jr. Fan Club members get weekly free Colby Ridge popcorn. Besides free admission for kids under 12, on Fan Club Night kids' activities may include car rides and coin or candy scrambles. Weekly go-kart racing is also popular, with participants as young as 5 competing.

Beyond racing, this "Edge of your seat entertainment" venue plans programs. Trailer races, Hillbilly Slip-n-Slides, firehouse rodeos, and even concerts have all happened. During the offseason, the track becomes Eagle Hollow—a premier scream park.

617 S. 238th St., Eagle, NE 68347
Office: (402) 238-2595
eagleraceway.com

TIP

Two area communities also have speedways: Greenwood's I-80 Speedway and McCool Junction's Junction Motor Speedway offer additional entertainment for racing fans.

ROLL A STRIKE
AT 48 BOWL

As Lincoln's BFF, 48 Bowl offers bowling, food, and fun. Offering two dozen lanes at each location, the 48 bowl can accommodate up to six people on each of the 48 automated lanes. With ramps, lifts, and bumpers, those of all ages and sizes can easily be a part of this indoor sport. Entertainment options light up during Parkway's Friday night Glo Zone bowling.

Throughout the week, discounts are available to make bowling even more affordable. Leagues for all ages are available at both locations. Having an event such because a birthday party is one of the best ways to introduce people to bowling as more fun is to be had with friends.

These locations also know their way around food. Legends Grill at Hollywood features pizza, salads, appetizers, and oven nachos. Fred's has operated its restaurant inside Parkway for over 50 years and is known for its burgers and sandwiches.

Hollywood Bowl	Parkway Lanes
920 N. 48th St.	2555 S. 48th St.
(402) 466-1911	(402) 483-7763

TIP
Although they are only open when school is session, the UNL East Campus Lanes N' Games is a smaller alley. For additional leagues and lanes, check out Madsen's Bowling and Billiards or Sun Valley Lanes.

BECOME
A HUSKER FAN

On fall football Saturdays, Memorial Stadium becomes Nebraska's third-largest city. Since 1962, every game has been sold out. Finding tickets can be challenging, yet attending a football game is an experience not to be missed even for non-football fans. For family fun, the Husker Nation Pavilion is opened (weather permitting) three hours before kickoff. With inflatables and activities, kids can be a part of the game-day experience.

Being a Husker involves more than just games. By taking a tour of Memorial Stadium and/or the Bob Devaney Center, fans get the opportunity to see "behind the scenes." Tours must be set up in advance. Contact the athletic department for available times and details.

The Nebraska JV team recruits members through the eighth grade. This provides youngsters with the opportunity to get free tickets for some of the smaller events. Emails connect fans to weekly happenings.

Memorial Stadium
One Memorial Stadium Drive
(402) 472-3333

Bob Devaney Sports Center
1600 Court St.

SEE SOME STARS
AT HYDE OBSERVATORY

On clear Saturday evenings, amateur astronomers are provided better views of the stars and other night objects in the Lincoln sky. To streamline the process, three high-powered telescopes are stationary, focused on three different spots for that evening. Astronomy enthusiasts volunteer their time to help visitors learn about what they are observing.

Besides viewing objects outside, programs are offered inside the visitor's center to tell more about what is currently visible in the night sky. Not all planets and constellations are visible year-round. Even the moon is highlighted and programs rotate monthly.

This is a family friendly activity as even younger ones can view the night sky. Programs are free and the center provides early winter hours and later hours from March to October.

3701 S. 70th St.
(South side of Holmes Park)
(402) 441-7094
hydeobservatory.info

TIP
To learn more about the night sky, consider joining the local Prairie Astronomy Club (prairieastronomyclub.org) for a low annual fee.

47

PRACTICE PUTTING
AT JIM AGER GOLF COURSE

One of the finest short golf courses of its kind was started in Lincoln during the 1960s and was named for longtime Lincoln Parks and Recreation Administrator Jim Ager. This nine-hole course is open from March to November. Golf teaches kids lessons that go far beyond how to avoid sand traps.

With holes ranging from 75 to 170 yards, the golf course can be fun for people of all skill levels. For those who want a bigger target, foot golf is an option. Balls are kicked into large depressions located near the original holes. Children can attend golf camps where plastic clubs and inflatables are available. With over 80 programs, everyone can find a suitable class.

This location is the perfect kid hangout center, with basketball courts, kid-friendly movies, and even an arcade with 80 free games. For those who want to stick with golf, becoming a Youth on Course member is recommended. For a $10 membership fee, kids can play at Jim Ager for $4 and the other Lincoln Municipal Golf Courses for only $5.

3761 Normal Blvd.
(402) 441-8963
lincolncitygolf.org

TIP
If you are wanting to play a full eighteen holes of golf, there are four public golf courses located across Lincoln. Check out lincolncitygolf.org for the hours and locations.

CHECK OUT
THE LINCOLN STARS

The United States Hockey League added the Lincoln Stars to its team lineup in 1996. This expansion league team includes young men under 20 who hope to play professionally someday. Every year, many players are drafted into the NHL or recruited for college teams. Community members are given a billeting stipend to host national and international players in their homes throughout the season. Players attend local schools.

The Ice Box seats 4,300 fans. Their enthusiasm has created one of the top five arena atmospheres in North America. Through the years, the pregame light show has drawn both national and international acclaim.

The Lincoln Stars organization wants to give back to the community. Through the Stars Foundation, an emphasis is placed on funding clean water, both locally and beyond. "Stars Give Back" sends players into the Lincoln area to volunteer for various community organizations.

1880 Transformation Dr.
(402) 474-7827
lincolnstars.com

TIP
If you are wanting to be a part of the ice skating action, Lincoln has two venues. John Breslow Ice Hockey Center has indoor skating, and the Railyard Ice Rink is open at various times during the winter for outdoor skating.

FUEL UP FOR RACING
AT THE MUSEUM OF AMERICAN SPEED

Although the Museum of American Speed opened in 1992, Bill "Speedy" Smith and his wife Joyce started collecting racing memorabilia decades earlier. Being involved with both hot-rodding and racing spurred their fascination with historic automotive artifacts.

With over 150,000 square feet of display space, the museum has three floors of fascinating finds for guests to explore. Due to the vastness of the collection, repeat visits are encouraged because exhibits rotate. From early antique automobiles to noteworthy racing machines to specific modified parts, car enthusiasts have plenty to see. Displays also include pedal cars, automotive toys, and classic lunch boxes.

Educational and family friendly activities have become a part of the focus. Events are planned for young people with the hope that passions will be fueled for automotive history, innovation, and technical skills. Hands-on opportunities are included in the programs.

599 Oak Creek Dr.
(402) 323-3166
museumofamericanspeed.com

SPIN A WHEEL
AT THE NATIONAL MUSEUM OF ROLLER SKATING

Hosting the 1962 USA Roller Skating Championships in Pershing Auditorium was such a success that Lincoln went on to host many future events. The community's reception toward skating was so positive that, in 1968, the Roller Skating Rink Operator's Association moved to Lincoln. Since 1980, the museum has displayed skating artifacts.

Besides having the largest collection of historic roller skates, additional artifacts, such as trophies, medals, and costumes, are displayed. Exhibits highlight artistic, inline, and even rink speed skating. Memorabilia from roller hockey and skating derbies are also highlighted.

Beyond skates, the collection features over 1,500 roller skating books and periodicals. Archives include more than 10,000 photographs and personal papers of those prominent in the skating industry. Because the collection continues to grow, displays are continually updated.

4730 South St.
(402) 483-7551
rollerskatingmuseum.org

PRACTICE SHOOTING
AT THE NEBRASKA GAME AND PARKS OUTDOOR EDUCATION CENTER

Before the Outdoor Education Center opened in spring 2014, there wasn't a place where people could sharpen both their archery and rifle skills. Indoor and outdoor ranges ensure that weather doesn't prohibit practice. With 3-D targets and a roving field course, practice conditions imitate real-life situations.

All ages and skill levels are welcome. Although some just need to practice before hunting, others enjoy shooting arrows or guns as a form of recreation. Because of the practice areas, patrons can get the training they need.

Hunter education is offered, as well as additional classes and day camps. The center also offers a Junior Olympic Archery Development Course. On occasion, sports tournaments also take place.

4703 N. 44th St.
(402) 471-6141
outdoornebraska.gov/outdooredcenter

TIP
Although the Outdoor Education Center is only place that offers both riflery and archery, several other local places offer them separately. For shooting, there are Big Shots Indoor Range & Gun Store, Deguns Firearms Sales & Service, as well as Thunder Alley Indoor Shooting Range. Prairie Bowman Archery is the perfect place to practice with a bow and arrow.

TAKE A HIKE
TO PIONEERS PARK NATURE CENTER

One of Lincoln's oldest parks has been preserving and restoring Nebraska's natural habitats for decades. Four hundred acres of prairie is protected. Because Salt Creek runs through the park, saline wetlands support unique plants and animals such as inland salt grasses and fairy brine shrimp. This location emphasizes Great Plains living things.

Two interpretative buildings allow interaction with nature. The original Chet Ager Center focuses on area woodland and wetland species. At the Prairie Building, guests can explore the grasslands. The new educational building will offer additional programming. Paths lead to Nebraska native outdoor animals that live on park land.

Eight miles of hiking trails include two suspension bridges. An outdoor play area encourages interaction with nature. The park is continuing to expand its reach as a part of the Prairie Corridor Project.

3201 S. Coddington Ave.
(402) 441-7895
lincoln.ne.gov/city/parks/naturecenter
prairiecorridor.org

CATCH A FLY BALL
AT THE SALTDOGS' HAYMARKET PARK

Naming Lincoln's professional baseball team was challenging. Over 1,000 names were submitted. Because the city was built on a salt basin, that part of the name makes sense. As for the dogs, a "man's best friend" image was projected.

In 2001, the Saltdogs joined the South Division of American Association of Independent Professional Baseball. While the league name is a mouthful, what the title indicates is that games are played against central teams from Texas all the way up into Canada. Haymarket Park is unique with its 4,500 seats and 4,000 berm (sideline) spots. Considered a park within a park, guests can access the entire stadium perimeter. This stadium features a prime playing field.

Off the field, players connect to the community through charitable events. Homer's Heroes allows disabled children to experience baseball with the players. Being a part of Lincoln matters to the team.

403 Line Drive Circle, Ste. A
(402) 474-BALL
saltdogs.com

TIP
If you are looking for more baseball games to watch, the historic Sherman Field at 225 South St. often has local games going on.

IMAGINE PIONEER PRAIRIES
AT SPRING CREEK PRAIRIE AUDUBON CENTER

Grasses swayed as far as the eye could see when pioneers first passed through Nebraska over 175 years ago. Engraved wagon ruts cement their presence. Today the Spring Creek Prairie Audubon Center's goal is to protect 650 acres that have never been plowed. An additional 200 acres have been protected.

On the property are several ecosystems, including tall grass prairie, ponds, riparian areas, and wetlands. Visitors can experience each type of habitat. Trails are open from sunrise to sunset.

At the visitor's center, students of all ages can learn about the area wildlife and plants. Before hiking, fully supplied backpacks are offered to help guide learners into discovery. Themes include art, writing, and bird-watching. Science gadgets, tools, and activities fill the packs with possibilities.

11700 SW 100th St.
Denton, NE 68339
(402) 797-2301
springcreek.audubon.org

SLIDE INTO SUMMER
AT STAR CITY SHORES AQUATIC CENTER

Mayor Mike Johanns gave up the honor of being the first one down the coral pink slide when Lincoln's aquatic center opened in May 1996. Nick, a local sixth-grader who picked the name for the center, convinced Johanns to let him go first. He was also given a one-year pass. Two slides, waterfalls, fountains, and more were included in Lincoln's first zero-entry pool.

Twenty years later, the slides were replaced with a tube slide and with one that included multiple loops. The play area was expanded for younger kids. Squeals result when the giant bucket tips over after being filled with water.

4375 S. 33rd Ct.
(402) 441-6670

TIP
Across town, kids can keep cool by jumping in puddles and running through multiple sprinklers. This free Trago Sprayground at 20th and U is a perfect place to splash around.
lincoln.ne.gov/city/parks/parksfacilities/pools

LINCOLN PUBLIC POOLS

Arnold Heights Pool
4000 NW 46th
(402) 441-7829

Ballard Pool
3901 N. 66th
(402) 441-7898

Belmont Pool
12th & Manatt
(402) 441-7826

Eden Pool
4400 Antelope Creek
(402) 441-7827

Highlands Aquatic Center
5511 NW 12th
(402) 441-7800

Irvingdale Pool
1900 Van Dorn
(402) 441-7828

University Place Aquatic Center
2000 N. 48th
(402) 441-7834

Woods Pool
33rd and J
(402) 441-7782

PONDER THE BEAUTY
AT SUNKEN GARDENS

Creating beauty out of rubbish is possible. In 1930, a former neighborhood dumpsite was transformed into this breathtaking garden space. Despite the Great Depression, the city committed its own funds to hire unemployed men for the project. Until additional shrubs and trees were planted to fill the surrounding space, this location was nicknamed "the rock garden."

Every year, the gardens have a particular theme. Concepts have varied from "Purple Rain" to "Thunderbird" to "Women of the World." Plant shades and selections are coordinated to achieve the specified look. In mid-May, volunteers gather to "Wake up the Beds." In November, locals gather again to "Put the Beds to Bed."

Through the "Paving the Path" program, loved ones can be memorialized on the brick pathways. Because of the lily ponds and cascading waterfalls, strolling through the gardens is a great way to unwind. Many celebrations, including weddings, happen here.

S. 27th St. and Capitol Pkwy.
(402) 441-8258

TREK THE TRAILS
AROUND TOWN

Since 1978, bike trails have been winding their way through the capital city—over 131 miles of crushed rock or hard surface trails, to be precise. Some of the pathways came about as a result of the "Rails to Trails" project. Other paths were created during highway projects. Along the way, the trails wind through parks, playgrounds, prairies, and other green space areas.

Many of these pathways connect at the Jayne Snyder Trail Center. Opened in 2012, the center is the gathering hub. Meetings, receptions, and celebrations are all held inside or in the outdoor commons area. City Council Member Jayne Snyder served Lincoln throughout her lifetime and, as a physical therapist and lifelong runner, she was active on the trails. Through her fundraising efforts, the area trails were expanded.

Trails: lincoln.ne.gov/city/parks/parksfacilities/trails
Bike Lincoln: lincoln.ne.gov/city/plan/bike
Jane Snyder Trails Center

CLIMB A WALL
AT THE UNL OUTDOOR ADVENTURE CENTER

In 1972, officials at UNL wanted to encourage students to enjoy the great outdoors. In the beginning, that consisted of a trip and an equipment rental program operating from a garage on campus. Today the campus Outdoor Adventure Center also includes a bike shop, equipment rental, and an off-site challenge course.

The mission of Outdoor Adventures is to engage individuals and groups in adventurous experiences for educational enjoyment and escape. Instruction options include the "Couch to 5.10" class, which teaches the skills needed to enjoy the climbing experience. Students can also sign up to take adventure trips.

All services are open to the public, with discounts offered to members. Watercraft rentals are a big hit during the summer. The indoor climbing walls offer both bouldering and rope climbing. To participate, individuals must be 5 or older. Family memberships are available and include membership for kids under 15. UNL students get one free climb per semester.

>930 N. 14th St.
>(402) 472-4777
>crec.unl.edu/oac

PLAY A MATCH
AT WOODS TENNIS CENTER

For over 50 years, Woods Tennis Center has been the place to play in Lincoln. Over time, the facilities have expanded. Now a dozen outdoor courts and half a dozen indoor courts are available for a low fee. Reservations are encouraged.

Partial and full scholarships are available for programs and both group and private lessons are offered. Classes take place across the city through the Lincoln Parks and Recreation Department.

For those looking for fun, cardio tennis is a great option. If players want to step up their game, many tournaments are available from the junior to adult level. Singles, doubles, and even triples competitions are offered. Leagues encourage consistent play. The wheelchair team is a reminder that tennis is accessible to almost anyone. In 2018, Woods Tennis Center was named the Missouri Valley Tennis Facility of the Year.

401 S. 33rd St., (402) 441-7095
woodstenniscenter.wordpress.com

TIP

"Tennis Buddies" help this game to be accessible for everyone. A tennis enthusiast is paired up with a player who has disabilities. Because tennis is a low-impact sport, people of all abilities can play. This is organized in conjunction with the Special Olympics Practices that occur weekly during the season at Genesis Health Clubs at 55th and Old Cheney. Although membership is required, this location also provides indoor courts.

CULTURE AND HISTORY

LEARN ABOUT BRYAN, LINCOLN'S POPULAR POLITICIAN, AT HIS FORMER FAIRVIEW FARM

William Jennings Bryan's hilltop country acreage was once outside of Lincoln. This three-time Democratic Presidential candidate lived in Fairview with his wife, children, and even grandchildren for nearly 20 years. When he was politically active, he often gave speeches from the front porch that was later enclosed.

This historic home is now surrounded by the Bryan Health East Campus. Bryan donated his surrounding acres for a hospital. For a time, Fairview housed nurses in training.

Today volunteer docents lead tours by appointment. The house has been restored to resemble how it looked when the Bryans lived there. In the basement, displayed artifacts include family photographs, political cartoons, and historic postcards. The double-sided desk is where Mr. and Mrs. Bryan worked together on his political projects.

1600 S. 48th St.
(402) 481-3032

VISIT ANOTHER CULTURE
AT THE GERMANS FROM RUSSIA MUSEUM

For hopes of a better life, many Germans moved to Russia starting in 1762. Hard times hit again, so members of this displaced group began relocating to the Midwest in the US. Many settled near Lincoln's south creek bottoms. They raised families and helped build the community.

The American Historical Society of Germans from Russia was formed in 1967 as a support system for this large immigrant population. The headquarters moved to Lincoln in 1973. On-site is a research and genealogical library. A collection of German-Russian migration documentation is the largest collection in the Western Hemisphere.

The Heritage Center provides background for this storied community. Artifacts tell the story of journeys to find a better life. During warmer weather, surrounding outbuildings are opened for guided tours into typical stores, homes, and churches that would have been a part of this German-Russian community.

631 D St.
(402) 474-3363
ahsgr.org

TOUR
THE GOVERNOR'S RESIDENCE

Opening in 1958, this is Nebraska's second governor's residence. With its overall symmetrical design and hipped roof, the architectural style is Georgian Revival. Elaborate gardens feature Nebraska native plants.

Only some of the residence's 27 rooms are open to the public. The five bedrooms are private, as well as several of the 12 bathrooms. Nebraska is symbolized throughout the house with corn carpet patterns and the capitol engraved on a shower door.

In the basement gallery, in conjunction with the Nebraska Arts Council, Nebraska artists are featured. On special occasions, guests can see the First Lady (and Gentleman) inaugural doll collection. Because the home is also considered an office, many events take place on-site.

For security reasons, not many governors' homes are open for tours. Nebraska's residence is open by appointment only. Tours must be arranged at least two weeks in advance.

1425 H St.
(402) 471-3466
governor.nebraska.gov/governors-residence

APPRECIATE
WHAT THE WEST HAS TO OFFER AT THE GREAT PLAINS ART MUSEUM

John and Betty Christlieb were Western art aficionados. Over several decades, whenever they traveled to major cities, they came home with a masterpiece. Counting it all took time: There were 175 bronzes, 160 paintings/drawings, and 50 additional pieces. They also owned a 400-volume Americana library. An unfortunate incident motivated them to donate their collection. The University of Nebraska-Lincoln (UNL) agreed to keep the pieces together and the UNL Great Plains Art Museum was launched.

According to Curator and Museum Director Ashley Hussman, "The museum's unique focus on the Great Plains ensures that visitors will always have the opportunity to learn something new about the diverse art, history, and environment of the region."

Since other pieces have been added to the collection, exhibits rotate. To assist in education, the Western books are considered part of the UNL library. This free gallery is open Tuesdays through Saturdays.

1155 Q St.
(402) 472-6220
unl.edu/plains/great-plains-art-museum

PIECE TOGETHER THE PAST
AT THE INTERNATIONAL QUILT MUSEUM

For years, Aris and Robert James acquired quilts. Nearly 1,000 pieces were gathered over time. Rather than storing them away, the University of Nebraska agreed to keep the collection intact. What resulted is a world-class museum. The careful eye will notice quilt symbolism throughout, including the fact that the reception hall is shaped like the eye of a needle.

One-hundred-thirty quilt guilds from three different countries contributed to what is now the world's largest collection. In order to represent all eras and genres, the pieces chosen vary. To protect each quilt's integrity, they can only be displayed once every 10 years.

Beyond viewing quilts, the museum is a study facility, complete with a library. The interactive wall is designed to connect visitors with quilts. Seeing parts of a quilt in process helps viewers to understand the significance of production.

Today the International Quilt Museum sends its quilts around the world.

1523 N. 33rd St.
(402) 472-6549
internationalquiltmuseum.org

TIP
More fabric displays can be found at nearby East Campus at the Robert Hillestad Textile Gallery.

READ LOCAL LITERATURE
AT THE JANE POPE GESKE HERITAGE ROOM OF NEBRASKA AUTHORS

In 1949, Lincoln librarians started setting aside books by Nebraska authors. The collection initially filled a shelf behind the reference desk. Today the Heritage Room is filled with over 14,000 books and other materials. Shelves contain manuscripts dating back to the 1800s. Vertical files provide information on authors and additional collections include audiovisuals and historic photographs. Because these items must be preserved, they can only be viewed in the room during open hours.

Determining what to keep in the assortment is challenging for curators. Nebraska Book Award Winners are on the shelves, as are multiple editions of key Nebraska authors such as Cather, Sandoz, Eiseley, Neihardt, and more. Gradually the library is trying to digitize both VHS and audio cassettes, as well as other fragile pieces.

Besides collecting materials, the Heritage Room connects readers to its resources through programs and book talks. The Ames Reading Series features local authors. Writer workshops are also offered.

Bennett Martin Library, Third Floor
136 S. 14th St.
(402) 441-8516
lincolnlibraries.org/heritage-room-of-nebraska-authors

LOOK AROUND
NEBRASKA'S STATEHOOD MEMORIAL, THE KENNARD HOUSE

When Secretary of State Thomas Kennard had his house built in 1869, he wanted to make a statement. As a show of good faith, he and other early Nebraska leaders constructed permanent homes to demonstrate that Lincoln truly was the capital. Today this is Lincoln's oldest building.

Reflecting design trends from that era, the Italianate Style included long, narrow windows and a square cupola tower. The Kennards lived at this address for a few decades. Later the home was used as a fraternity or sorority, a boarding house, and a private boys' home.

When the house became state property, restoration was sorely needed. Rather than recreating Kennard's home, the Nebraska Historical Society staff returned both the exterior and interior back into a typical Victorian-style house. Tours are now available by appointment. On the day of the capitol Christmas tree lighting, the home is open to treat visitors to a Victorian Christmas.

1627 "H" St.
(402) 471-4764
history.nebraska.gov/visit/thomas-p-kennard-state-historic-site

TIP
Next door, the Ferguson House is open to the public on a very limited basis, available for rental for events, and an annual holiday open house. 700 S. 16th St., (402) 471-5417

ACT LIKE A FARMER
AT LARSEN TRACTOR TEST AND POWER MUSEUM

Buying tractors in the early days was a risky venture. Machines were not standardized and guarantees were limited. After multiple tractor brand breakdowns, Nebraska farmer Wilmot Crozier was fed up. Upon his election to the legislature, he put tractor testing laws in place.

Nebraska has the only tractor testing facility in North America. Those who stop by on testing days can observe the multi-step process and experts and students are on hand to explain everything.

Inside the museum, the collection demonstrates the history of testing equipment, including a workshop display. Exhibited tractors vary in size, make, and model and kids can enjoy a scavenger hunt. Retired tractor enthusiasts or student volunteers are often on hand for tours. Admission is free, but donations are appreciated.

1925 N. 37th
(near Fair St.)
(402) 472-8389
tractormuseum.unl.edu

TIP
If you would like to experience what a farm was like in 1920s Nebraska, take a short drive out to Wessels Living History Farm near York.

APPRECIATE MASTERPIECES
AT KIECHEL FINE ART GALLERY

The Kiechel family wanted to bring fine art to Nebraska. Since 1986, this local gallery has specialized in 19th and 20th century American art, as well as old master and contemporary prints. To expand its offerings, it has worked consistently with particular artists and collectors. Pieces from the gallery's collection have found their way into private and public collections worldwide.

The collection of regional art is unparalleled and 10 area artists are frequently highlighted. Exhibits rotate to display more of the gallery's collections. To educate patrons, the Kiechel website is a source of art history.

Beyond purchasing masterpieces, clients can request art consultations and certified appraisals. Protected art storage is another option. For those looking for a grand space to host a gathering, the gallery can be rented for exhibitions or events.

1208 "O" St.
(402) 420-9553
kiechelart.com

OTHER LINCOLN ART GALLERIES

Burkholder Project
719 "P" St.
(402) 477-3305
burkholderproject.com

**Elder Gallery at
Nebraska Wesleyan**
5000 St. Paul Ave.
facebook.com/
NWUElderGalleru

**Eisentrager-Howard
Art Gallery at UNL**
120 Richards Hall
(402) 472-5522
facebook.com/EHArtGallery

Gallery Nine
124 S. Ninth Street
(402) 477-2822
gallerynine.com

Metro Gallery
1316 "N" St., No. 101
(402) 202-7549
metrogallerynebraska.com

Noyes Art Gallery
119 S. Ninth St.
(402) 475-1061
noyesartgallery.com

Tugboat Gallery
116 N. 14th St.,
(402) 477-6200
tugboatgallery.com

**Midwestern African
Museum of Art**
1936 "Q" St.
(402) 438-0529
africaculturecenter
-museum.org

69

BE REMEMBERED
AT THE KINDLER HOTEL

Nebraska native Ken Kindler worked with HVAC by day and crafted unique metal garage art at night. Some of his pieces are displayed in this boutique hotel that Nick and Brooke Castaneda named in honor of her father. Other Lincoln area artists are also featured. Connecting to the local community is emphasized and creating a downtown haven for Lincoln visitors is the mission.

Because there are only 49 rooms, customer connection is key. Personalized hospitality is emphasized. Suites and standard rooms are available. Designer Ross Vincent had all of the furnishings custom-crafted to reflect a Modern Deco theme.

Former Olympic skater and current television chef Brian Boitano crafted signature Nebraska-themed and other original cocktails for his Boitano's Lounge. An executive chef offers a seasonal small plates menu. Nearby, Ivanna Cone provides signature ice cream flavors. Diners are encouraged to linger.

216 N. 11th St., (402) 261-7800

TIP
If you prefer to stay at chain hotels, two locations have a uniquely Lincoln flair. Since 1926, people have been lodging at the Cornhusker Hotel, now Lincoln Marriot Cornhusker. At the Graduate Lincoln, décor features many Nebraska elements including corn wallpaper and Koolaid mustache art.

70

FEEL APPRECIATION
AT THE CITY OF LINCOLN FIREFIGHTER AND RESCUE DEPARTMENT MUSEUM

In 1886, the Lincoln Fire Department transitioned from an all-volunteer department to a paid force. At that time, there were two stations that shared a hook-and-ladder truck, a hose cart, a steamer, and a chief's buggy. Now that there are 16 stations, both the equipment and the firefighters have multiplied.

In 1982, a museum room was added to Fire Station No. 1. Equipment is displayed, along with photographs from the department's history. About 20 years later, displays were rearranged in chronological order to allow visitors to better understand the fire department's storied past.

The centerpiece of the museum is the 1911 pumper truck. Another unique artifact is an old breathing apparatus consisting of wooden bellows and a leather mask. Also displayed is the company's first bulky, portable, 3-foot radio.

The museum is open daily and firefighters often give the tours. If station personnel are out on calls, be prepared to wait. Community safety comes first.

1801 Q St. (Station No. 1)
(402) 441-8360

CREATE
AT LUX CENTER FOR THE ARTS

Gladys Lux taught art in northeast Lincoln for decades. Nebraska Wesleyan students were recipients of her expertise. Her goal was to make art accessible. In 1977, the University Place Art Center began. Ten years later, Gladys purchased the former University Place City Hall and donated it to the center, which was then renamed. Today LUX Center for the Arts is dedicated to transforming lives through art.

Throughout the year, at least 18 exhibitions of local, regional, and national artists are presented in five gallery spaces. In the carefully curated shop, patrons can buy and gift art. Classes are available in ceramics, painting, drawing, glass, mixed media, and metals/jewelry.

Outreach is an important part of the center. Schools with low-income children are a focus. Art experiences are also created for the elderly and for the incarcerated. Complete with discounts, memberships are a wonderful way to support this center.

2601 N. 48th St.
(402) 466-8692
luxcenter.org

UNCOVER A FOSSIL
AT MORRILL HALL

Greeting visitors to the state's natural history museum is Archie, the giant bronze mammoth. Although natural history artifacts have been collected since early university days, Morrill Hall's opening in 1927 was the first time the items were together. Nebraska's natural history is celebrated at this museum.

Presented are ancient Nebraska fossils as well as preserved Nebraska plants and wildlife. "First People of the Plains" tells the stories of Nebraska's Native Americans. Only parts of the massive research collections, which include multiple branches of science, are displayed. Gallery programs and Mueller Planetarium shows expand scientific knowledge for visitors.

In the Marx Discovery Center, kids get to play around with science. Hands-on exhibits celebrate biodiversity. Nebraska's Ashfall Fossil Beds are recreated, so kids can uncover a rhinoceros fossil with paintbrushes and pretend tools.

645 N. 14th St.
(402) 472-2637
museum.unl.edu

73

EXPERIENCE
THE NEBRASKA CAPITOL

Nebraska's third capitol stretches higher than all other Lincoln buildings. Walk around the exterior promenade to see the story of democracy carved in stone. All of Nebraska's 93 counties are also inscribed.

Interior tours occur hourly and are highly recommended. The symbolism and meaning of this building is staggering. From the floor and ceiling mosaics to the centennial artwork, every space tells a story. All three branches of Nebraska's government are in the Capitol: the Governor's Suite, the Supreme Court chambers, and the unicameral legislature.

Ride up the elevator to the 14th floor to get a bird's-eye view of Lincoln. On nicer days, the doors are open to allow for better viewing. The inside Memorial Chamber celebrates Nebraskans' contributions to society.

1445 K St.
(402) 471-0448
capitol.org

UNDERSTAND
THE STATE'S PAST
AT THE NEBRASKA HISTORY MUSEUM

Even before Nebraska became a state, the land left behind artifacts. In 1983, the Nebraska History Museum was opened to put those items on display and catalog over 150 years of history.

Since the museum has over 125,000 objects available, displays are rotated. Topics have included Nebraska archeology, cowboys, women's suffrage, cars, photography, and more. These exhibits are meant to be interactive.

To further connect with the community, events are planned. "School's Out" days are offered during school breaks and summer vacation. Hands-on activities allow students to experience educational concepts in a fun way. "Free Family Fun Days" take place Saturday afternoons and connect with current exhibits. Scavenger hunts are often a part of both experiences.

The Brown Bag Lecture Series is held monthly. Guest experts present Nebraska history over a lunch hour. Unless noted, admission is free to the museum and events. Donations are appreciated.

131 Centennial Mall N.
(402) 471-4754
facebook.com/nebraskahistorymuseum

GO UNDER LINCOLN
AT ROBBER'S CAVE

Depending on tradition, Lincoln's original cave was named for the city, the penitentiary, or the Pawnee Council Cave. Legends abound. Robber's Cave was determined to be the final name due to its possible use as a hideout. Once a quarry, then expanded into a brewery, the cave was also a transient camp before becoming a tourist attraction.

Groups held gatherings inside the cave. Many organizations are familiar, but the Hoot Owl Club, Military Order of the Cootie, Palladium Literary Society, and the West Oak Sewing and Cooking Club disappeared long ago. Groups loved the intrigue of the cave's passageways.

Musical groups appreciated the acoustics, and bands like The King Bees and Charlie Brown's Generation performed there. UNL football parties and square dances filled the caverns. Possibly the most memorable event was the Flintstones-themed birthday party that included a buffet for 200 guests.

Today local expert Joel Green leads cave tours. Reservations must be made in advance. Explore Lincoln's underground tunnels that are filled with stories.

925 Robbers Cave Rd.
(402) 975-0598
robberscavetours.com

VALUE
SHELDON MUSEUM OF ART

For decades, an assortment of art pieces from the University of Nebraska were scattered in various buildings and smaller galleries. Architect Philip Johnson, known for his Glass House, applied his design perspective to create the University's Sheldon Museum of Art in the 1960s to house the collection. Over time, the collection grew to 13,000 pieces. Large-scale sculptures are on permanent display across campus. Interior exhibits rotate frequently to allow for varied viewing. Sheldon Statewide allows communities across Nebraska to temporarily display pieces as well. Most of the collection can be seen online.

Being on a university campus necessitates an educational approach to art. Instructional events happen at various times. These gatherings tell the stories of art to the community. Admission is free and the museum is open almost every day.

12th and R
(402) 472-2461
sheldonartmuseum.org

STAY IN THE CITY
OR STAY IN THE COUNTRY

Rogers House Inn

This former retired banker's 1914 home has been a bed and breakfast since 1984. A recent ownership change has brought new life to the historic home while preserving its integrity. Offerings include five standard bedrooms and two suites. The Banker's Suite, the original owners' winter quarters, includes a fireplace and sitting area. The signature breakfast dish is the blueberry ingot, a delectable cake.

Besides offering overnight accommodations, the Rogers House hosts events. From baby showers to holiday gatherings, the spacious main floor is perfect for celebrations. Catering is also available.

2145 B St., (402) 476-6961, ww.rogershouseinn.com

Prairie Creek Inn Bed & Breakfast

Bruce and Maureen Stahr felt drawn to save the Leavitt House. After purchasing the vacated Veteran's Administration hospital building, they moved the 1911 structure to the country. Only the exterior was left intact. They spent several years rebuilding the interior. Six bedrooms now welcome guests, with two floors open for gatherings.

Additionally, the 1900 Cottage House and Lake Lodge can be rented. All are B&B accommodations and include breakfast. The inn's signature dish is the Spanish tortilla. The original barn, now known as Opry Barn, has been updated to host gatherings, including receptions, square dances, and concerts.

2400 S. 148th St., Walton, NE, (402) 488-8822, pcibnb.com

OTHER LINCOLN AREA BED AND BREAKFASTS

Burgess House Bed & Breakfast
6501 SW 40th St.
(402) 797-2345
burgesshousebb.com

Westview Bed & Breakfast
7000 NW 27th St.
(402) 470-6000
westviewbb.com

Wunder Roost Bed & Breakfast
14817 S. 25th
Roca, NE 68430
(402) 430-9130

STROLL THROUGH HISTORY
AT WYUKA CEMETERY

Meaning "resting place" in Lakota, Wyuka is Lincoln's oldest existing cemetery. Established in 1869, this is a rare official state cemetery and, because so much of Lincoln's history is visible on the stones, a book is devoted to its exploration.

Several Nebraska governors and significant Lincoln citizens were laid to rest at Wyuka. In the middle is a veterans' tribute. Graves date back to the Civil War and white crosses lining the hill are a reminder of sacrifice. A portion of the plots are designated for Jewish citizens. On the eastern side is the Nebraska Holocaust Memorial, featuring a "Wall of Remembrance."

Inside the Rudge Memorial Chapel, small funerals and even weddings are conducted. The renovated original stables now host gatherings. Once, the grounds were a picnic destination. Today swans are in the pond and the manicured lawns again provide a beautiful place to rest.

To learn more, please read Lincoln historian Ed Zimmer's *Wyuka Cemetery: A Driving and Walking Tour* guide. The PDF version is available to download from history.nebraska.gov.

(402) 474-3600
wyuka.com

79

HONOR THE MILITARY
AT VETERANS MEMORIAL GARDEN

The traveling Vietnam Memorial was once set up in a ballfield at Antelope Park and it changed the park forever. Between that 1989 event and increased patriotism with the Gulf War, the Lincoln community is determined to show its support of the military. Today that field is the Veterans Memorial Garden. Thirty-seven memorials, monuments, and tribute benches honor those who served.

This outdoor memorial is the perfect place to introduce kids to the cost of freedom. Because so many branches and conflicts are featured, history is brought to life. Donated by loved ones, Bricks of Honor are stark reminders that each one has his or her own story.

On patriotic holidays, community gatherings are often held. On those occasions, the garden commands attention as 46 American flags wave proudly. The commemorative ceremonies celebrate Veterans' contributions to helping the United States to continue to be "the land of the free and the home of the brave."

1650 Memorial Dr.
(402) 441-7847
facebook.com/LNKVeteransGarden

TIP
Antelope Park is one of Lincoln's largest gathering places. The City of Lincoln worked with local high school students and donors to construct a fully integrated, accessible play area in Antelope Park for children of all abilities.

SHOPPING AND FASHION

SHOP TOGETHER
AT 3 DAUGHTERS BOUTIQUE

Some of Stephanie Johnson's fondest memories growing up were shopping with her mom and two sisters. When she had three daughters of her own, she continued the tradition. Upon facing an empty nest, she decided that she wanted to retire from her stock broker business and pursue her personal passion: fashion.

Stephanie's goal is for every woman to have a positive shopping experience. That is why her business is "passionate about helping women see the good in themselves, one fabulous outfit at a time." Since 2016, the boutique has displayed clothes that will suit women from ages 18 to 88.

Half of the items carried are made in the US. Half are also produced by women-owned companies. Relationships with customers and companies matter.

Giving back is important to the owners. The boutique frequently donates clothing and store gift cards to local charitable organizations that support women and the community, such as the Friendship Home.

311 N. 8th St., Ste. 102
(531) 289-1411
facebook.com/3daughtersboutiqueLincoln

ADDITIONAL LOCAL LINCOLN BOUTIQUES

Ash & Ash Co.
7301 S. 27th St., Ste. 110 & 120
(531) 500-6093
6900 "O" St., Ste. 116
(402) 261-8337
ashandashco.com

BeKá Boutique
4702 Prescott Ave., Ste B
(402) 610-1049
bekaboutiqueclothing.com

Forever Faithful
321 N. Eighth St.
(402) 435-0662
facebook.com/
foreverfaithful.ofe

The Nines in Fallbrook
575 Fallbrook Blvd.
(402) 904-5257
facebook.com/
theninesfallbrook/

Ruby Begonias
1321 P St.
(402) 438-4438
instagram.com/rubybegonias/

Stella Clothing
101 N. 14th St., Ste. 7
(402) 476-0028
facebook.com/
stellaclothingstore/

81

CULTIVATE IDEAS
AT CAMPBELL'S NURSERY & GARDEN CENTER

Claude Campbell lived near the last trolley stop. Because his house was along the walking route to Wyuka Cemetery, many noticed his beautiful gardens and began asking to purchase flowers for gravesites. This railway mail sorter became a horticulturist.

By relocating, his family was able to purchase land for growing. His wife and son wrapped pansies, tomatoes, and peppers in newspapers and sold from their backyard. After the war, Claude's son, Bob, joined the company. Their 40th Street acreage was once at the edge of town and allowed them to add trees and other plants. They eventually added additional land, which again allowed them to expand.

Today Campbell's nursery includes third-fourth-generation family members. Longtime employees also contribute to their success. By offering quality products and providing gardening assistance, the business has continued to grow. Many clients return each year to enjoy the nursery's landscape design services.

5625 Pine Lake Rd.
(402) 423-4556

Campbell's Garden Center
2342 S. 40th
(402) 483-7891

ADDITIONAL LOCAL LINCOLN FLORISTS

Abloom Florist
1451 O St., No. 100
(402) 435-6937
abloomlincoln.com

Burton & Tyrrell's Flowers
3601 Calvert, Ste. 12
(402) 421-2613

Fields Floral
3845 S 48th St.
(402) 483-4564
fieldsfloral.com

Flowerworks
6900 O St.
(402) 325-6900
flowerworksonline.com

Gaga's Greenery & Flowers
2626 N. 48th St.
(402) 464-8266
gagasgreenery
andflowers.com

House of Flowers
6940 Van Dorn St., No. 100
(402) 476-2776
house-of-flowers.com

Nebraska Nursery & Color Gardens
4420 Lucille Dr.
(402) 489-6543
colorgardens.com

Oak Creek Plants & Flowers
3435 S. 13th St.
(402) 421-2999
oakcreekflowers.com

Petals to Platinum
440 N. Eighth St., No. 130
(402) 817-4771
petalstoplatinum.com

82

POP UP MEMORIES
THROUGH COLBY RIDGE

When Donn Steinbach was laid off from his engineering position, he checked around with friends to see if anyone had an opening. The family who owned Korn Popper offered him a job. Within the first week, not only was he making the product, he was ordering supplies and doing clerical work. Three months later, when he was offered his old job back, the Korn Popper family begged him to stay and buy their business. Thanks to the support of family members, Donn became the owner in 1983.

Two years later, Donn opened his second store and named it Colby Ridge. Now there are several storefront locations. Gourmet white is the best seller. Specialized flavors vary and include caramel apple and cheesy jalapeño. Tins, gift boxes, and other varieties of this Nebraska-grown product are available.

6940 Van Dorn St.
(402) 489-9116

4822 Pioneers Blvd.
(402) 489-0149

colbyridgepopcorn.com

TIP
If you are in other parts of Lincoln, Simply Amaizen Popcorn & Snacks (simplyamaizenpopcorn.com) offers snacks at two locations. Topper Popper has been a long Northeast Lincoln favorite as well.

ALTER YOUR LIFE
AT EMSUD'S CLOTHIERS

When the Deumics arrived in the United States from Bosnia, all they had was clothes and each other. Shortly before coming to the US, Samka and her children were reunited with her husband, Emsud, after his time in a concentration camp. Thanks to the support of Lincoln's First-Plymouth Church, they left that refugee camp. Starting over in the United States was a dream come true.

Emsud's family has a strong tradition in the tailoring and clothing business. After having a few jobs in Lincoln in that field, he started Emsud's Expert Alterations in 1998. A year later, they all became citizens. Through hard work, his kids (Alma and Salko) finished college, and the family bought a home.

Soon they expanded to add retail services, especially men's clothing. Their current 8,000-square-foot location is another dream come true because they own the land and the building. The business is still family operated and they still do alterations. Providing suits for purchase to wedding parties is a new avenue. Most of all, customers are greeted with a smile from a grateful family.

5525 Red Rock Ln.
(402) 420-7288, emsuds.com

TIP
Watch for advertisements of famous athletes wearing clothing from a local store, Gary Michaels Clothiers, another longtime Lincoln tradition.

84

DESIGN YOUR DREAM
AT COOPER & CO.

Diane Cooper has always loved decorating. Knowing how to combine elements makes all the difference. For many years Diane operated the Basket Bunch, a specialty gift shop, but in 2015 she decided to go a different direction.

Cooper and Co. focuses on transforming houses into homes. Now her daughters, Shane Olson and Natalie Lundgren, are adding their skill sets to the store. Their involvement is Diane's favorite part of this new concept. A wide range of decorating services is available.

There is a reason they were voted Lincoln's best furniture store. Between affordable accessories and quality pieces, their welcoming selection fits a variety of styles and tastes. Their 20,000 square feet of showrooms provide plenty of possibilities to help customers create spaces that reflect who they truly are.

2211 Winthrop Rd.
(402) 904-8192
cooperandcolincoln.com

TIP
If you are looking for other types of gifts, check out these other local favorites: Good Things, Plum Creek Gifts, and Paper Kite.

PLAY AN INSTRUMENT
AT DIETZE MUSIC

August Dietze started his store in 1925 with the goal of connecting the Lincoln area with music. During the store's long history, Dietze has always provided a full line of music resources. This approach is rare across the country.

One of the store's strengths is its many employees who are music educators. When instruments are purchased and rented, instruction is available. With the repair shop, technical support is offered. Offsite, the Dietze Music Room at the Lincoln Children's Museum creates musical play opportunities. The goal is to develop the next generation of music makers.

Beyond selling instruments, Dietze is committed to being involved in the community. The company provides sound technicians as well as stage sponsorships for many charitable events that include music. In appreciation of the support that Lincoln has provided its company, Dietze Music wants to pay its success forward.

5555 S. 48th St.
(402) 704-8265, (866) 391-3336

6401 Q St., (402) 858-1039
dietzemusic.com

TIP
Palmer's Music Store (palmersmusicstore.com) and Roots Music Shop (rootsmusicshop.com) also offer musical experiences.

BE FOOTLOOSE
& FANCY

On a mid-1970s California trip, the McCabes noticed a lady selling sandals out of her trunk. Margo Frasier had dozens of Birkenstocks. She sent multiple pairs back home with the Nebraska couple and asked the McCabes to send her a check once they sold them. As a result of this whimsical encounter, the McCabes started Footloose & Fancy, one of the first US stores to sell the German shoes.

Twenty years later, Jane Stricker started working at the store. She eventually purchased it with her husband, Matt, and they later started an additional location. Other products were added, including clothing. At that point, they added "Threads" to their logo.

Outdoor-themed products from sustainable companies are sold. Shoes can be re-corked and re-soled. Environmentally friendly is key. Benefiting customers' lives is the focus. This family owned company contributes to community causes as well.

1219 P St.
(402) 476-6119

4131 Pioneer Woods Dr.
(402) 488-6119

threadsfootloose.com

TIP
If you are looking for a bigger shoe selection, check out the local Pattino Shoe Boutique located at 3943 S. 48th St.

LASSO
YOUR INNER COWBOY AT THE FORT

Volunteer firefighter Carl Wohlfarth and wife Shirley, a nurse, wanted to support their kids' interest in horses. Because there wasn't a Lincoln tack store back in 1972, they started one. Besides saddles, the shack included feed. Then a Tony Lama sales representative asked if they would consider selling boots. The possibilities only expanded from there.

Today the Fort is a full-service western store. Tack is still available and quality Western wear for work and for play are also available. "Fort Frontier" brand are items specific to the store. Shooter and range boots are available and, for the little cowpokes, miniature tractors and frontier toys are offered.

Over time, four locations have been added. Their mail order option expanded the business. The Fort has gained a national following as customers fly from other states to shop there. Singer Garth Brooks is among many such satisfied buyers.

Alamo No. 4
5601 S. 56th St.
(402) 421-3678
fortbrands.com

TIP
If you happen to be walking around Gateway Mall, look for Western World. This is another Lincoln original that features Western wear.

FROM NEBRASKA
GIFT SHOP

For over 30 years, buying Nebraska-made products has been possible at this delightful Haymarket shop. When ownership changed hands, the shop added James Arthur Vineyard wine tastings. Gift boxes were also added to highlight some of the best products the state has to offer.

Because Nebraska is the largest popcorn producer in the US, many varieties are offered, including some that pop on a cob in the microwave. Unique corn on the cob jelly is one of the many jams. Nebraska honeys include lavender, smoky, and pepper flavors.

Thanks to a local screen printer, original T-shirts are offered with a variation of the state's current slogan, "Nebraska, It's Not for Everyone." Clothing products exhibit a whimsical take on our great state. Official Lincoln shirts from the Convention and Visitor's Bureau are also available.

For products to be included, a direct connection to Nebraska is necessary. Packaging matters. New vendors are added if they offer a unique item or approach that is not already available at the store.

803 Q St.
(402) 476-2455
fromne.com

COOK GOURMET
AT HABITAT

Mary Clark was on a mission. She wanted Lincoln to have the same household offerings that were found in bigger cities. Habitat opened in 1975—the year her son, John, went off to kindergarten.

At first, Habitat sold products ranging from dinnerware to crystal to mixing bowls, operating from the Gunny's location at 13th and Q streets. Then Clark began offering gourmet food items, kitchen gadgets, household décor, and more. Habitat changed locations but continued to offer a high level of customer service.

John moved back to help with the store and soon reconnected with a longtime high school friend, Jana. Soon they were joined both personally and professionally. Jana's experience as a gift buyer added a new element to the store.

Over time, the store has continued to pay attention to the trends. Because the operators can respond quickly to customer requests, they are able to customize their service. Their unique assortment of merchandise continues to set Habitat apart.

4107 Pioneer Woods Dr., No. 112
(402) 466-1522
habitatgift.com

FIND A TREASURE
AT FUNKY SISTER

Debbe Andrews credits her late husband, Terry, with inspiring her to dream big. Back when they raised four children together, funds were limited. When Terry passed away after a brief battle with cancer, she moved forward with her dream of starting a store with prices accessible to everyone by opening the Funky Sister in 2015.

Inside the 100-year-old building, the items on sale are an equal mix of new, old, and repurposed. Family members have supported her vision. In particular, Debbe's daughter, Katie, helps bring her upcycled visions to life. For instance, a ladderback chair was missing a leg. Two legs became the framework for lamps, and the other became a candlestick. The back became a towel rack, and the seat is waiting for inspiration. For Debbe, part of the fun is finding new life for pieces to tell a story.

4724 Prescott Ave.
(402) 525-7805
thefunkysister.com

OTHER ANTIQUE STORES

Conner's Architectural Antiques
1624 S. 17th St.
(402) 435-3338
connersarchitectural
antiques.com

Aardvark Antique Mall
5800 Arbor Rd.
(402) 464-511

Antique Corner Cooperative
1601 S. 17th St.
(402) 476-8050
antiquecorner
cooperative.com

Burlington Antiques
201 N. 7th St., Ste. 102
(402) 475-7502
burlingtonantiques.com

Flatwater Toys
105 N. 8th St., Ste. 101
(402) 440-4803
flatwatertoys.com

C Middleton Antiques & Uniques
1615 S. 17th St.
(402) 477-1331
cmiddletonantiques.com

Cool and Collected Antiques
3235 S. 13th St.
(402) 435-1779
coolandcollected
antiques.com

A Street Antiques
4431 N. 62nd St.
(402) 474-5272

Modern Vintage
1366 S. 33rd St.
(402) 937-8712
modernvintagenebraska.com

Scherer's Architectural Antiques
9141 S. 63rd St.
(402) 423-1582
antiquesbrickandstone.com

SUPPORT LOCAL PRODUCERS
AT THE HAYMARKET FARMERS MARKET

In Lincoln's early days, the western edge of the community was filled with produce. In 1985, area farmers decided to revisit that concept by setting up stalls where city dwellers could purchase fresh, local produce. On Saturday mornings from May through mid-October, old brick streets are lined with vendors.

Organic vegetables, fruits, locally processed meats, and flowers are offered. Standard food fare includes baked goods like kolaches and pies, as well as breakfast burritos, wood-fired pizzas, mixes, specialty drinks, and wine. Handmade items range from blankets to T-shirts to wreaths to jewelry to yard art.

Live bands perform from around 9:30 to 11 a.m. Iron Horse Park is the gathering space. To keep shoppers safe, all weapons, animals and promotional materials must be kept at home. For many in Lincoln, attending the Farmer's market is a weekly tradition.

Seventh and Eighth St., from "P" to "Q" Streets

OTHER FARMERS MARKETS

Fallbrook Farmers Markets (Thursdays)
570 Fallbrook Blvd.
(308) 216-0411
facebook.com/fallbrookfarmersmarket

The Little Red Farm
577 S. Fourth Rd.
Palmyra, NE 68418
(402) 601-1208
thelittleredfarm.com (check website for hours)

Sunday Farmers Market at College View
4801 Prescott Ave.
(402) 318-5225
sundayfarmersmarket.org

Open Harvest Co-op Grocery (open daily)
1618 South St.
(402) 475-9069
openharvest.coop

FIND A NEW PASTIME
AT HOBBYTOWN

When Chick Bartlett started his downtown Lincoln store in 1946, he wanted to remind people to play. His original offerings included model trains, planes, gas engines, stamps, coins, and "dinky" toys. Later, three friends purchased his version of HobbyTown and then offered franchises.

Today they have over 100 locations in multiple states. Franchise are a part of the "HobbyTown Nation." Every year these owners are invited to attend a family reunion to rejoice in achievements and to enjoy each other's company.

Every store provides opportunities for guests to engage minds and hands. Multiple classes offer the community a chance to gather. Face-to-face fun is emphasized.

For those wanting to create projects from home, there is a variety of interactive possibilities. Legos are a popular item. Finding a meaningful pastime is easy at HobbyTown.

4107 Pioneer Woods Dr., Ste. 108
(402) 434-5040

3255 Cornhusker Hwy., Ste. B5
(402) 261-6714

hobbytown.com

MORE LINCOLN LOCATIONS THAT ENCOURAGE CREATIVITY

Art & Soul
5740 Hidcote Dr.
(402) 483-1744
lincolnartandsoul.com

Cosmic Cow
6136 Havelock Ave.
(402) 464-4040
cosmiccowfabricsandquilting.com

Gomez Art Supply
120 N. 14th St.
(402) 477-6200
gomezartsupply.com

Makit Takit: Lincoln's Craft Studio
4720 Prescott Ave.
(402) 483-4232
makittakit.com

Pages in Time Scrapbook/Mixed Media Store
5221 S. 48 St.
(402) 420-6933
facebook.com/Pages-in-Time-ScrapbookMixed-Media-Store-163263483767076

93

DECK YOURSELF IN RED
AT HUSKER HEADQUARTERS

When you sell Husker gear, having your grand opening during football season is wise. Especially if your promotional giveaway involves tickets. Since 2000, this local store has been offering big red clothing, accessories, and even home décor. One popular item is the signature cornhead hat.

Being located blocks from the stadium is an added bonus. For many who come to Lincoln on football Saturdays, the game-day experience is not complete without a stop at the store. Someone is usually around to talk about the season. Personal connections lead to many repeat customers.

The selection is so unique that the store is frequented not only by loyal fans but also by Husker coaches and players. If you prefer to avoid parking downtown, two other stores are open in Lincoln.

1120 P St.
(402) 438-8800

5631 S. 56th St.
(402) 423-8805

6100 O St. (Gateway Mall)
(402) 904-7116

huskerheadquarters.com

TIP
For even more Husker memorabilia, check out these additional local spirited stores: Best of Big Red (bestofbigred.com) and Nebraska Sports.

SHOW YOUR PERSONALITY
AT JILLY'S SOCKS

Lori Goff was known for being a great teacher and for her silly socks. Wearing fun socks provided her with another way to connect with her students. After three decades in education, she wanted a change of pace. Initially, she considered a new career in real estate before stepping into a special sock store while on a trip. She and her husband became passionate about the idea of starting their own store in Lincoln.

The business is named for a former student who was a part of the store's beginning. Lori's daughter-in-law, Kim, and the rest of the family have continued to support the effort. Repeat customers and former students who are now employees are the important backbone of Lori's business.

As for the store, almost any type of sock is available. More than that, other local businesses provide an assortment of goods as well. Lori's favorite is Chuck's Birdhouses—creations made by her dad. Stop by for the socks, shop the other selections, and stay for the conversations.

3900 Old Cheney Rd., Ste. 202
(402) 261-8308
jillyssocks.com

95

TRY A SAMPLE
AT LICORICE INTERNATIONAL

An elderly woman's love for licorice, a Manhattan man's desire to retire, and collaboration among four longtime friends resulted in Licorice International's Lincoln arrival. At first, the mail-order company operated from a basement, then on Prescott Avenue. Next, stop was the Haymarket. The wives became "The Licorice Ladies," with the husbands helping out on occasion.

In 2019, the couples wanted to retire. Who better to take over than a sweet young lady who had worked at the business for 16 years? The next chapter for this candy company is Erin's story. Locals can try her homemade nut rolls, salted taffy, and fudge.

As for the licorice? That is still the bulk of the store. Fifteen countries are represented with over 160 types, varying from salty to sweet. While they carry other flavors, only black is considered licorice. The Haymarket Store also sells gelato.

A second store opened in College View and both places provide samples and continue to add sweetness to Lincoln.

4725 Prescott Ave. (College View)
230 N. Seventh St. (Haymarket)
1-800-Licorice
licoriceinternational.com

MORE LOCAL SWEET TREATS

Chocolate Season: Chocolaterie & Espresso Bar
3855 Village Lane, Ste. 100
(402) 466-1139
thechocolateseason.com

Tasty Good Toffee
tastygoodtoffee.com

Sweet Minou (Tiny Fine Chocolate Factory)
sweetminou.com

96
READ A CLASSIC
AT A NOVEL IDEA BOOKSTORE

A Novel Idea Bookstore, located downtown for three decades, is a bi-level shop full of used, rare, and out-of-print books, with everything from paperback mysteries to leather-bound books signed by presidents.

Tops of the custom-made shelves are carved to look like leaves and some shelves have inset tiles. There are stained glass windows. The staircase, painted to look like old books, leads to a room with a flagstone floor. The stock rotates constantly and there are always small stacks of books waiting to be shelved.

Resident cats, Eddy and Charlie, often sleep in the front windows but love to snuggle and play with customers. Owner Cinnamon Dokken jokes that they are the most popular staffers, but she and her longtime manager, Kat Bergstrom, are better at recommending books. The (human) staff will help you find the perfect read!

118 N. 14th St.
(402) 475-8663
anovelideabookstore.com

MORE LOCAL USED BOOK STORES

Badgers Bookshop
4730 Cooper Ave., (402) 314-6602
facebook.com/Badgers-Bookshop-432720110249701/

Bluestem Books
137 S. Ninth St., (402) 435-7120
bluestembooks.com

LOCAL STORE FEATURING NEW BOOKS

Francie & Finch Bookshop
130 S. 13th St., (402) 781-0459
francieandfinch.com

PREPARE FOR AN ADVENTURE
AT THE MOOSE'S TOOTH

Lincoln's original outfitting store opened in 1983 and it's not just the owners who love all things adventure. Moose's Tooth employees are expected to have experience in exploring. Because they are highly active people, they can help customers pick the products that truly fit what they want.

The store offers an assortment of climbing, backpacking, and trekking equipment. To be included, products must have a lifetime warranty through the manufacturer. Camping items are waterproof. Everything sold must be either repairable or replaceable. While this does result in a higher price tag, when tent poles can be easily replaced and the broken pieces mended, the extra cost is worth it.

Cycleworks is owned by the same family. This shop started across the street with a handful of books and some accessories in a former car wash. Still today, their emphasis is quality. Bikes purchased here include a lifetime adjustment warranty.

Moose's Tooth
moosestooth.com, (402) 475-HIKE

Cycle Works
Cycleworksusa.com, (402) 475-2453

Both at 720 N. 27th St.

MORE BIKE AND OUTDOOR SHOPS

The Bike Rack
3321 Pioneers Blvd.
(402) 488-2101
bike-rack.com

**Method Cycles
& Craft House**
416 S. 11th St.
(844) 807-7035
methodcycles.com

Polkadot Bicycles
3863 South St.
(402) 730-1820
polkadotbicycles.com

Salty Dog Cyclery
1640 "O" St.
(402) 464-2453
saltydogcyclery.com

Wheelie Good Bike Shop
5633 S. 16th St., No. 400
(402) 261-8854
wheeliegoodbikeshop.com

LOAD UP ON ADVENTURE
AT STAR CITY MOTOR SPORTS

This store started in 1963 as Randolph Cycle and Marine. Ownership changed hands and so did the name. Robert Kay purchased Star City Motor Sports in 1997. Due his successful ascent up Mt. Everest, his nickname is the "world's top motorcycle dealer."

Because of the store's longevity, it is able to offer multiple new and used brands under one roof. Customers can pick the brands that fit their personal styles. Star City sells opportunities. By offering motorcycles, ATVs, motorbikes, Jet Skis, and more, each customer can choose his or her own adventure. To be certain of their purchase, customers can test drive the machines. Top brands include Honda, Kawasaki, Suzuki, Yamaha, CanAm, SeaDoo, Polaris, and Roxor.

By keeping five technicians on staff, Star City helps customer keep their purchases running. Amateur mechanics can also order parts and fix their own machines. With a full lineup of accessories and a location near the interstate, Star City Motor Sports is the starting point for outdoor fun.

6600 N. 27th St.
(402) 474-7777
starcitymotorsports.com

99

SMELL LINCOLN SCENTS
AT WAX BUFFALO CANDLES

Her daughter's birth caused Alicia Reisinger to reprioritize. Because her baby had a cleft lip and palette, treatment was needed. During this time, Alicia rediscovered a lost love. Candles connected her to her grandma. Tea parties with her grandmother included votive candles. Alicia's first candle, cinnamon-scented for Christmas, was a gift to that special lady.

Her form of therapy soon turned into an opportunity. Gifts made for friends turned into requests for more. By using pure soy wax high-end phthalate-free oils, the cleaner-burning candles were safe for all households and production started in her kitchen. After she moved to the Haymarket, retail sales and candle-pouring classes were added. Standard and seasonal scents are for sale, along with a curated monthly subscription box.

Alicia appreciates partnering with other women business owners and offers several of their products in her store. A valued connection with customers is made during collaborative candle events.

727 "O" St.
waxbuffalo.com

TIP
You can support Feya Candles, another local Lincoln maker, by ordering from their online-only store at feyacandle.com. For every candle purchased, this company donates a meal to a child in need.

100

LACE UP PERFECT SHOES
AT THE LINCOLN RUNNING COMPANY

According to the shelves, the point seems to be selling shoes. Yet Lincoln Running Company employees know the point is more than footwear. By listening and paying attention, customers leave with comfortable shoes that will be used rather than sit in the closet.

When the owners started the store back in 1976, running was becoming a craze. Today their grandson owns the shop, and local running enthusiast Ann Ringlein, is the longtime manager. Ringlein helped start the Lincoln Track Club and the shop has sponsored many races.

Training is offered through the store. Classes are available for beginning to more advanced runners. Information is also presented to help athletes recognize when they are just feeling sore or are actually injured and need to seek medical help. Those who feel hesitant about running will soon have the skills to cross the finish line.

1213 Q St.
(402) 474-4557
lincrunningcompany.com

TIP
If running is not your thing, the local Body Basics (nebraskafitnesssmart.com) and Let's Talk Bowling offer equipment for other sports.

SUGGESTED ITINERARIES

DATE NIGHTS
Read a Classic at A Novel Idea Bookstore, 128
Be Remembered at the Kindler Hotel, 92
See a Show at Pinewood Bowl, 51
Twirl Around at the Pla More Ballroom, 53
Slow Down Dinner at Prairie Plate, 26
Become a Film Critic at Mary Riepma Ross Media Arts Center, 55
Nosh in the Neighborhood at Toast, 27

NIGHT ON THE TOWN
See a Live Show at Bourbon Theatre, 41
See Some Stars at Hyde Observatory, 65
Be a Spectator at Pinnacle Bank Arena, 52
Twirl Around at the Pla More Ballroom, 53
Nosh in the Neighborhood at Toast, 27
Elevate Your Expectations at Zipline Brewing Co., 36

GIRLS DAY
Shop Together at 3 Daughters Boutique, 106
Something for Everyone at Goldenrod Pastries, 6
Take a Sip at James Arthur Vineyards, 12
Show Your Personality at Jilly's Socks, 125
Smell Lincoln Scents at Wax Buffalo Candles, 133

GUYS DAY OUT

Watch Cars Go in Circles at Eagle Raceway, 62

Bite a Big Burger at Honest Abe's, 10

Practice Shooting at the Nebraska Game and Parks Outdoor Education Center, 70

Load Up on Adventure at Star City Motor Sports, 132

Elevate Your Expectations at Zipline Brewing Co., 36

FAMILY OUTINGS

Putt a Hole in One at Adventure Golf, 60

Smile, You're at Champions Fun Center, 42

Solve a Puzzle at Escape Room Lincoln, 43

Roll a Strike at 48 Bowl, 63

Scream out Ivanna Cone, 9

Play Like a Kid at the Lincoln Children's Museum, 46

Feed the Goats at the Lincoln Children's Zoo, 47

Take in Local Theater at Lincoln Community Playhouse, 48

Paint Yourself Silly, 50

Celebrate Fall at Roca Berry Farm, 54

Sing With Your Supper at Screamers Dining and Cabaret, 56

Slide into Summer at Star City Shores Aquatic Center, 74

Trek the Trails Around Town, 77

GETTING READY FOR A FAMILY NIGHT AT HOME

Pop Up Memories Through Colby Ridge, 110

From Nebraska Gift Shop, 116

Cook Gourmet at Habitat, 117

Find a New Pastime at HobbyTown, 122
Read a Classic at A Novel Idea Bookstore, 128
Taste the Tradition at Valentino's, 34

CELEBRATING LINCOLN'S HISTORY
Feel Appreciation at the City of Lincoln Firefighter and Rescue Department Museum, 93
Uncover a Fossil at Morrill Hall, 95
Understand the State's Past at the Nebraska History Museum, 97
Go Under Lincoln at Robber's Cave, 98
Try Beef and Cabbage Sandwiches at Runza, 28
Chomp on Complimentary Chips and Salsa at Tico's Restaurant and Tequila Bar, 32

SPORTING ADVENTURES
Cheer for Teams Together at Gate 25 Bar and Restaurant, 4
Become a Husker Fan, 64
Practice Putting at Jim Ager Golf Course, 66
Catch a Fly Ball at the Saltdogs' Haymarket Park, 72
Check Out the Lincoln Stars, 67

CULTURED COMMUNITY
Appreciate Masterpieces at Kiechel Fine Art Gallery, 90
Read Local Literature at the Jane Pope Geske Heritage Room of Nebraska Authors, 87
Listen Closely to Lincoln's Symphony Orchestra, 49
Value Sheldon Museum of Art, 99

ACTIVITIES
BY SEASON

SPRING

Sing Along at Abendmusik at First-Plymouth, 40

Cultivate Ideas at Campbell's Nursery & Garden Center, 108

Practice Putting at Jim Ager Golf Course, 66

Lace Up Perfect Shoes at the Lincoln Running Company, 134

Imagine Pioneer Prairies at Spring Creek Prairie Audubon Center, 73

SUMMER

Watch Cars Go in Circles at Eagle Raceway, 62

Lasso Your Inner Cowboy at the Fort, 115

Scream out Ivanna Cone, 9

Support Local Producers at the Haymarket Farmers Market, 120

Take a Sip at James Arthur Vineyards, 12

Jazz in June, 44

Feed the Goats at the Lincoln Children's Zoo, 47

Catch a Fly Ball at the Saltdogs' Haymarket Park, 72

Slow Down Dinner at Prairie Plate, 26

Go Under Lincoln at Robber's Cave, 98

Slide into Summer at Star City Shores Aquatic Center, 74

Ponder the Beauty at Sunken Gardens, 76

Act Like a Farmer at Larsen Tractor Test and Power Museum, 89

Trek the Trails Around Town, 77

FALL

Play an Instrument at Dietze Music, 113

Bite a Big Burger at Honest Abe's, 10

Deck Yourself in Red at Husker Headquarters, 124

Feel Appreciation at the City of Lincoln Firefighter and Rescue Department Museum, 93

Celebrate Fall at Roca Berry Farm, 54

WINTER

Find a New Pastime at HobbyTown, 122

Piece Together the Past at the International Quilt Museum, 86

Show Your Personality at Jilly's Socks, 125

Play Like a Kid at the Lincoln Children's Museum, 46

Check Out the Lincoln Stars, 67

Stay Caffeinated at The Mill, 20

Paint Yourself Silly, 50

INDEX

(402) Creamery, 9
3 Daughters Boutique, 135
48 Bowl, 63
9 South Char Grill, 15
A Novel Idea Bookstore, 128
A Street Antiques, 119
Aardvark Antique Mall, 119
Abendmusik at First-Plymouth, 40, 138
Abloom Florist, 109
Adventure Golf, 60, 136
Ali Baba Gyros, 22
Amigos, 29
Antelope Park, 51, 103
Antique Corner Cooperative, 119
Arnold Heights Pool, 75
Aroma Indian Cuisine, 13
Art & Soul, 123
Ash & Ash Co, 107
Asian Fusion, 3
Backswing Brewing Co., 37
Badgers Bookshop, 129
Bagels & Joe, 19
Ballard Pool, 75
Bánhwich Café, 2
Bay, The, 61
Be Footloose & Fancy (Threads), 114
BeKá Boutique, 107

Belmont Pool, 75
Best of Big Red, 124
Big Sal's Pizza and Wings, 17
Big Shots Indoor Range & Gun Store, 70
Bike Rack, The, 131
Billy's Restaurant, 25, 35
Blue Orchid Thai Restaurant, 3
Bluestem Books, 129
Bob Devaney Sports Center, 64
Body Basics, 134
Boiler Brewing Company, 37
Bourbon Theatre, 41, 135
Braeda Fresh Express Café, 28
Brewskys, 5
Burgess House Bed & Breakfast, 101
Burkholder Project, 91
Burlington Antiques, 119
Burton & Tyrrell's Flowers, 109
Butterfly Bakery, 7
C Middleton Antiques & Uniques, 119
Cactus: Modern Mexican & Catina, 25
Camp Sonshine, 54
Campbell's Garden Center, 108
Campbell's Nurseries & Garden Center, 108

Capitol View Winery
   & Vineyard, 12
Cappy's Hot Spot Bar and Grill, 5
Carmelo's Bistro and Wine Bar, 15
Champions Fun Center, 42, 136
Chocolate Season: Chocolaterie &
   Espresso Bar, 127
Code Beer Company, 37
Coffee House, The, 21
Colby Ridge, 62, 110, 136
Conner's Architectural
   Antiques, 119
Cookie Company, 7
Cool and Collected Antiques, 119
Cooper & Co., 112
Copal Progressive Mexican
   Cuisine, 33
Cosmic Cow, 123
Cosmic Eye Brewing, 37
Cupcakes & More, 7
Cycle Works, 130
D'Leons, 29
daVinci's, 17, 42
DelRay Ballroom, The 53
Deer Springs Winery, 12
Deguns Firearms Sales & Service
   Shooting Range, 70
Dietze Music, 113, 139
Dino's, 15
Dish Restaurant, 25
Doughnut Hole, The, 31
Eagle Raceway, 62, 136, 138
Eatery, 31

Eden Pool, 75
Eisentrager-Howard Art
   Gallery at UNL, 91
El Chaparro, 33
El Rancho, 33
El Toro, 33
Elder Gallery at Nebraska
   Wesleyan, 91
Empyrean Brewing Co., 14, 37
Emsud's Clothiers, 111
Engine House Café, 8
Escape Room Lincoln, 43, 136
Fairview Farm, 82
Fallbrook Farmers Markets, 121
Farmers Market at College
   View, 121
Ferguson House, 88
Feya Candle, 133
Fields Floral, 109
Fireworks, 14
Flatwater Toys, 119
Flowerworks, 109
FlyDogz, 29
Forever Faithful, 107
Fort, The, 15, 138
Francie & Finch Bookshop, 129
From Nebraska Gift Shop, 116, 136
Funky Sister, 118
Gaga's Greenery & Flowers, 109
Gallery Nine, 91
Garage Sports Bar/Grill, The, 5
Gary Michaels Clothiers, 111

Gate 25 Bar and Restaurant, 4–5, 137
George's Gourmet Grill Downtown, 22
Germans from Russia Museum, 83
Goldenrod Pastries, 6, 61, 135
Gomez Art Supply, 123
Good Evans, 31
Good Things, 112
Governor's Residence, 84
Graduate Lincoln, 92
Grata Bar and Lounge, 15
Gratitude Café and Bakery, 7
Great Plains Art Museum, 85
Great Wall Chinese Restaurants, 3
Green Gateau, 19
Greenfield's Restaurant, 31
Ground Up, 10–11
Habibi Kabob and Schwarma, 22
Habitat, 117, 136
Hacienda Real, 33
Hacienda Real Highlands, 33
Harbor Coffeehouse, 21
Haymarket Farmers Market, 120, 138
Haymarket Park, 72, 137–138
Haymarket Theatre, 48
HF Crave, 11
High Society Cheesecake, 7
Highlands Aquatic Center, 75
HobbyTown, 122
Hollywood Bowl, 63
Honest Abe's, 10–11
House of Flowers, 109
Hub Café, The, 26
Husker Headquarters, 124, 139
Huskerville Pub and Pizza, 17
Hyde Observatory, 65, 135
I-80 Speedway, 62
Imperial Palace, 3
International Quilt Museum, 86, 139
Irvingdale Pool, 75
Isles Pub and Pizza, 8
Issara Cuisine, 3
Ivanna Cone, 9, 92, 136, 138
James Arthur Vineyards, 12, 116, 135, 138
Jane Pope Geske Heritage Room of Nebraska Authors, 87, 137
Jane Snyder Trails Center, 77
Jazz in June, 44, 138
Jilly's Socks, 125, 135, 139
Jim Ager Golf Course, 66, 137–138
John Breslow Ice Hockey Center, 67
John Shildneck Memorial Bandshell, 51
Joyo Theater, 55
JTK Cuisine and Cocktails, 15
Junction Motor Speedway, 62
Junto Wine, 12
Kennard House, xiii, 88
Kiechel Fine Art Gallery, 90, 137
Kindler Hotel, 92
La Paloma, 33

La Paz, 33
Lanes N' Games, 63
Larsen Tractor Test and Power Museum, 89, 139
Las Margaritas, 33
Lazlo's Brewery and Grill, 14
Lazzari's Pizza, 16
Le Quartier Baking Co., 18
Lead Belly, 27
Lee's Chicken, 35
Let's Talk Bowling, 134
Licorice International, 126
Lied Center, The, 45, 49
Lincoln Children's Museum, 44, 46, 113, 136, 139
Lincoln Children's Zoo, 47, 136, 138
Lincoln Community Playhouse, 48, 136
Lincoln Escape Room, 43
Lincoln Espresso, 21
Lincoln Firefighter and Rescue Department Museum, 93, 137, 139
Lincoln Marriot Cornhusker Hotel, The, 92
Lincoln Running Company, 134, 138
Lincoln Stars Hockey, 67
Lincoln Youth Symphony, 49, 137
Lincoln's Symphony Orchestra, 49
Little Red Farm, The, 121
Lost in Fun, 42

LUX Center for the Arts, 94
M & J's Southern Style Food, 25
Madsen's Bowling and Billiards, 63
Makit Takit: Lincoln's Craft Studio, 123
Mary Riepma Ross Media Arts Center, 55, 135
Mazatlan, 33
Mazatlan II, 33
Memorial Stadium, 4, 64
Method Cycles & Craft House, 131
Metro Gallery, 91
Midwestern African Museum of Art, 91
Mill Coffee & Bistro at Nebraska Innovation Campus, 20
Mill Coffee & Tea at College View, The, 20
Mill Coffee & Tea at Telegraph, The, 20
Mill Coffee & Tea in the Historic Haymarket, The, 20
Ming's House, 3
Misky Bakery, 7
Misty's Steakhouse and Lounge, 8
Mo Java Café & Roasting Company, 21
Modern Vintage, 119
MoMo's Pizzeria and Ristorante, 17
Moose's Tooth, 130
Morrill Hall, 95, 137
Museum of American Speed, 68
N Zone Sports Bar & Grill, The, 5

National Museum of Roller Skating, 69
Nebraska Capitol, 96
Nebraska Game and Parks Outdoor Education Center, 70, 136
Nebraska History Museum, 97, 137
Nebraska Nursery & Color Gardens, 109
Nebraska Sports, 124
Nines in Fallbrook, The, 107
Nitro Burger, 11
Normandy, 19
Noyes Art Gallery, 91
nuVibe (Juice & Java), 21
Oak Creek Plants & Flowers, 109
Open Harvest Co-op Grocery, 121
Oven, The, 13
Pages in Time Scrapbook/Mixed Media Store, 123
Paint Yourself Silly, 50, 136, 139
Palmer's Music Store, 113
Pancho Villa Mexican Grill, 33
Paper Kite, 112
Parkway Lanes, 63
Parthenon Greek Grill and Taverna, 22
Pattino Shoe Boutique, 114
Penelope's Lil' Café, 31
Petals to Platinum, 109
Peter Pan Park, 61
Phat Jack's, 23
Pho Factory, 3
Piedmont Bistro by Venue, 24–25

Piezano's, 17
Pinewood Bowl, 51, 135
Pinnacle Bank Arena, 4, 52, 135
Pioneers Park Nature Center, 71
Pla Mor Ballroom, 53
Plum Creek Gifts, 112
Polkadot Bicycles, 131
Prairie Bowman Archery, 70
Prairie Creek Inn Bed & Breakfast, 100
Prairie Plate, 26, 135, 138
Press Box Sports Bar & Grille, 5
Rabbit Hole Bakery, The, 7
Railyard Ice Rink, 67
Ramos Pizza/Buster's BBQ and Grill, 17
Randy's Donuts, 31
Risky's Sports Bar and Grill, 5
Robber's Cave, 98, 137–138
Robert Hillestad Textile Gallery, 86
Roca Berry Farm, 54, 136, 139
Rococo Theater, 41
Rogers House, 100
Roots Music Shop, 113
Rosie's Sports Bar, 5
Royal Grove, The, 41
Ruby Begonias, 107
Runza, xiii, 28, 137
Saigon Plaza, 2–3
Saltdogs, 72
Salty Dog Cyclery, 131
Scherer's Architectural Antiques, 119

Screamers Dining and Cabaret, 56, 136
Sebastian's Table/Eleanora Bar, 11
Sheldon Museum of Art, 44, 55, 99, 137
Shen Café, 3
Simply Amaizen Popcorn & Snacks, 110
Single Barrel, The, 15
Spikes Beach Bar and Grill, 5
Sportscasters Bar and Grill, 5
Spring Creek Prairie Audubon Center, 73, 138
Stage Theater, The, 48
Star City Motor Sports, 132, 136
Star City Shores Aquatic Center, 74, 136, 138
Stauffer's Café and Pie Shoppe, 30
Stella's Clothing, 107
Stur 22 Lounge, 15
Sultan's Kite, 22
Sun Valley Lanes, 63
Sunken Gardens, 76, 139
Super Taco, 33
Sweet Minou, 127
Taco Inn, 29
TADA Theater, 48
Tandoor, 13
Taqueria El Rey, 33
Tasty Good Toffee, 127
Theatre Arts for Kids, 48
Thunder Alley Indoor Shooting Range, 70

Tico's Restaurant and Tequila Bar, 32, 137
Tierra Briarhurst Park, 61
Tina's Café and Catering, 35
Tiru Ethiopian Restaurant, 22
Toast, 27
Tomahawks Ax Throwing, 43
Topper Popper, 110
Trails Tugboat Gallery, 91
University Place Aquatic Center, 75
UNL Dairy Store, 9
UNL Outdoor Adventure Center, 78
Valentino's, 34
Venue Restaurant and Lounge, 24–25
Veterans Memorial Garden, 103
Virginia's Travelers Café, 31
Warm Cookie, The, 7
Wax Buffalo, 133, 135
Wessels Living History Farm, 89
Western World, 115
Westview Bed & Breakfast, 101
Wheelie Good Bike Shop, 131
White Elm Brewing Co., 37
WindCrest Winery, 12
Woods Pool, 75
Woods Tennis Center, 79
Wunder Roost Bed & Breakfast, 101
Wyuka Cemetery, 102, 108
Yia Yia's, 17
Zipline Brewing Co., 36, 135–136
Zoo Bar, 57